THE TASTE OF OUR TIME

Collection planned and directed by

ALBERT SKIRA

BIOGRAPHICAL AND CRITICAL STUDY

BY

MAURICE RAYNAL

Translated by James Emmons

CÉZANNE

SKIRA

CHRONOLOGICAL SURVEY

1839 Birth of Paul Cézanne at Aix-en-Provence, January 19. The family hailed from a village named "Cézanne" (Cesena) on the Italian side of Mont Genèvre, but was of French stock.

1841 Birth of Renoir, Bazille, Berthe Morisot.

1847 His father took over the Banque Barges, then in the process of liquidation, and with a partner launched it as a new concern, the Banque Cézanne et Cabassol.

1848 Birth of Gauguin.

1849 Day-boarder at the Pensionnat Saint-Joseph at Aix.

1852 Boarder at the Collège Bourbon. Thorough classical education, backed by religious teaching. Amongst his schoolfriends were Baptistin Baille and notably Emile Zola; with the latter he remained very intimate until their quarrel in 1886.

1856 Works under Gilbert at the Aix School of Drawing, where he wins a second prize in 1858. Also studies music; much enthusiasm for Wagner. Fond of country walks with Baille and Zola.

1859 Takes his degree in Letters. Begins his correspondence with Zola. His wish is to go to Paris to study painting, but his father insists on his entering the Law School at Aix. In this year Cézanne père, whose bank is prospering, buys a country house near Aix, "Le Jas de Bouffan," where young Cézanne spends the summer and sets up a studio.

1859 Birth of Seurat.

1860 He tries to persuade his father to let him devote himself to painting, and his mother and sister Marie back him up in this. Besides Zola and Baille, with whom he subsequently loses touch, his friends at this time are the sculptor Philippe Solari (his faithful friend until his death), who did his bust in 1904, Numa Coste, who became a journalist, Achille Emperaire, a painter, and Anthony Valabrègue, an art-critic. Is now influenced by Loubon and the paintings in the Caravaggio manner in the Aix Museum.

1860 Great success of Courbet at the Salon.

1861 April. His father gives in at last and goes with him to Paris. He lodges Rue des Feuillantines and attends the Académie Suisse, where he meets Guillaumin and Pissarro; the latter greatly influences him. Visits the Louvre and Salon. September. After a setback at the Ecole des Beaux-Arts, has a fit of homesickness, goes back to Aix and takes a post in his father's bank, though he still attends drawing classes in the evening. He now does murals at Le Jas de Bouffan: "The Four Seasons," "Interior" (Museum of Modern Art, Moscow), inspired by prints in a fashion magazine.

1861 At the age of 81 Ingres paints "Le Bain Turc." Manet shows for the first time at the Salon.

1862 Returns to Paris in November, where he remains until 1864. Works at the Académie Suisse. Becomes very friendly with Pissarro, Guillaumin, Oller, Guillemet, Bazille, Monet, Sisley, Renoir. With Zola visits the 1863 Salon des Refusés. He still admires above all Delacroix and Courbet. Embarks on a series of intensely romantic works.

1862 Degas paints his first pictures of horse races and jockeys.

1863 Exhibition of Modern Painting at Martinet's. Sharp attacks on Manet for his "Déjeuner sur l'herbe" at the Salon des Refusés. Death of Eugène Delacroix.

1864 Cézanne again loses heart and returns to Aix. From 1864 to 1870 shares his time between Paris and Aix. The pictures he sends into the Salon are invariably rejected. At Aix from July 1864 to the beginning of 1865.

1864 Birth of Toulouse-Lautrec.

1865 Manet exhibits "Olympia" at the Salon.

1866-1867 Rejected at the 1866 Salon, Cézanne dispatches a letter of protest to the Director of Fine Arts. Introduced to Manet, who admires his still lifes. Does portraits of Valabrègue, Emperaire, and his father reading "L'Evénement," the newspaper that published Zola's first articles on Manet.

1867-1869 Long stays in the South. When in Paris, constantly moving. Baroque compositions with erotic tendencies. "The Rape," "The Orgy," "The Temptation of St Anthony."

6

1867 The Goncourt brothers publish "Manette Salomon." Birth of Bonnard. Death of Ingres and Baudelaire. Monet's "Women in the Garden." Exhibition of work by Courbet and Manet.

1869 At Etretat Courbet paints "The Wave." Renoir and Monet work together at Bougival. The impressionist technique takes form. Birth of Matisse.

1870 During the Franco-Prussian war Cézanne lies low at L'Estaque, near Marseilles, where he lives with Hortense Fiquet, his wife-to-be.

1871 The Paris Commune. Birth of Rouault.

1873 Settles down at Auvers-sur-Oise, where he stands on friendly terms with Dr Gachet. Paints "The Hanged Man's House" and several landscapes showing Pissarro's influence. Meets the dealer known as Père Tanguy.

1874 Takes part in the First Impressionist Exhibition thanks to Pissarro's good offices, and despite the opposition of the other exhibitors. His canvases, a landscape at Auvers, "The Hanged Man's House" and "A Modern Olympia," were those most derided by the public.

1875 Makes friends with Chocquet.

1875 First impressionist sale at the Hôtel Drouot. Death of Corot.

1876 Spends the summer at L'Estaque. Refuses to join in the Second Group Exhibition of the Impressionists.

1877 Works at Pontoise and Auvers. Shows 17 canvases at Third Group Exhibition (still lifes and landscapes), but the public is more hostile than ever.

1877 Death of Courbet.

1878 Retires to L'Estaque. Cuts loose from Impressionism.

1878 Paris World's Fair. Duret publishes "Les Peintres impression-nistes."

1879 Again rejected at the Salon.

1879 Death of Daumier.

1880 Lives in Paris from February of this year until May 1881. Makes Huysmans' acquaintance. Spends the summer with Zola at Médan.

1880 Death of Flaubert.

1881 Works with Pissarro at Pontoise from May to October. Short stay at Aix in November.

1881 Birth of Picasso.

1882 Renoir visits him at L'Estaque. Accepted at the Salon as "Guillemet's pupil." Stays in Paris from February to September, then settles at the Jas de Bouffan near Aix.

1883 Works in the neighborhood of Aix, then at L'Estaque from May to November with Monticelli. In December Renoir and Monet pay him a visit.

1883 Death of Manet.

1884 Founding of the Salon des Indépendants.

1885 With Renoir at La Roche-Guyon. Returns in August to the South, where he stays until 1888. Works chiefly at Gardanne, a small town perched on a hilltop some six miles outside Aix. The "classical" element in his style is growing more and more pronounced.

1885 Pissarro meets Signac and Seurat; adopts Pointillism in 1886. Van Gogh at Nuenen.

1886 Marries Hortense Fiquet in April. Breaks with Zola, who in his novel "L'Œuvre" modeled one of the characters, an unsuccessful painter, on Cézanne. His father dies, settling a comfortable fortune on him.

1886 Van Gogh comes to Paris, meets Lautrec. Eighth and Last Impressionist Exhibition. Degas shows a set of pastel nudes. Revelation of the Douanier Rousseau at the Indépendants. Gauguin's first stay at Pont-Aven in Brittany. Rimbaud publishes his "Illuminations."

1887 Exhibits with "Les Vingt" at Brussels.

1887 Birth of Juan Gris and Marc Chagall. Mallarmé publishes his "Poésies complètes."

1888 A short stay in Paris. Country rambles in the Ile-de-France.

1888 Van Gogh at Arles. Gauguin's second stay at Pont-Aven with Emile Bernard: Cloisonnism and Synthesism. James Ensor paints "The Entrance of Christ into Brussels."

1889 Cézanne entertains Renoir at the Jas de Bouffan. Shows at the "Décennale" exhibition at the Paris World's Fair, but only after Chocquet intercedes in his behalf.

1889 Paris World's Fair. Construction of the Eiffel Tower. Verlaine publishes "Parallèlement," and Bergson his "Données immédiates de la conscience." Gauguin stays at Pont-Aven, then at Le Pouldu, where he paints his "Yellow Christ." Van Gogh enters the Saint-Rémy Asylum, near Arles.

1890 Death of Van Gogh. Launching of the "Mercure de France."

1891 A pleasure trip to Switzerland and the Jura region. First attack of diabetes.

1891 Van Gogh Retrospective Exhibition at the Salon des Indépendants. Bonnard exhibits for the first time. Death of Seurat. Gauguin leaves for Tahiti. The Natanson brothers launch the "Revue Blanche." First exhibition of the Nabis.

1892 Stays at Fontainebleau. To the early nineties, an extremely fertile period, belong the 5 versions of "The Card Players," the series of "Baigneuses," and that of the "Montagne Sainte-Victoire."

1892 Seurat Retrospective Exhibition in the offices of the "Revue Blanche." Matisse arrives in Paris and enrolls at the Académie Julian.

1893 Opening of the Vollard Gallery in Paris. Matisse and Rouault meet. Birth of Miró.

1894 Cézanne spends the autumn at Giverny in the home of Monet, who introduces him to Rodin, Clemenceau, Gustave Geffroy.

1894 Caillebotte Bequest to the Musée du Luxembourg.

1895 Cézanne's first one-man show at Ambroise Vollard's. His work is cold-shouldered by the public, but thought much of by artists and some connoisseurs. "Portrait of Gustave Geffroy" and "Boy with the Red Waistcoat."

1895 First public motion-picture shows given by the Lumière brothers. Gauguin leaves a second time for Tahiti. Publication of Rimbaud's "Poésies complètes," with a preface by Verlaine.

1896 Makes the acquaintance of the young poet Joachim Gasquet, who becomes one of his warmest admirers.

1897-1898 Paints some fine views of the Valley of the Arc overhung by Montagne Sainte-Victoire. He rents a cottage at the Bibemus quarry, above the Aix barrage. Death of his mother on October 15, 1897. Visits Paris.

1897 "La Revue Blanche" publishes Gauguin's manuscript "Noa-Noa," while in Tahiti Gauguin paints his vast composition "Whence come we? What are we? Whither go we?" The Caillebotte Bequest is at last accepted by the State.

1898 Death of Stéphane Mallarmé.

1899 Sells the Jas de Bouffan. Exhibits three canvases at the Salon des Indépendants.

1899 Group Exhibition of the Nabis at Durand-Ruel's. Signac publishes "D'Eugène Delacroix au Néo-Impressionnisme." Death of Sisley.

1900 Cézanne figures at the Centennial Exhibition: his fame is on the increase, abroad as well as in France. The National-galerie in Berlin purchases one of his pictures. Maurice Denis paints his "Homage to Cézanne."

1900 Paris World's Fair. Seurat Retrospective Exhibition organized at the "Revue Blanche" by Félix Fénéon. Picasso's first stay in Paris.

1901 Exhibits at "La Libre Esthétique," Brussels, and also at the Indépendants. Buys some land on the Les Lauves road north of Aix and has a studio built on it.

1901 Death of Lautrec. First Picasso exhibition at Vollard's; meeting with Max Jacob; beginning of his Blue Period. Apollinaire comes to Paris. Van Gogh exhibition at Bernheim's.

1902 The death of Zola, despite their break, is a great blow to Cézanne. Octave Mirbeau tries to secure his nomination to the "Légion d'Honneur," but fails.

1902 Picasso exhibits at Berthe Weill's and at Vollard's. Matisse exhibits at Berthe Weill's.

1903 Death of Gauguin. Gauguin Memorial Exhibition at the Salon d'Automne.

1904 Stays some weeks at Paris and Fontainebleau. An entire room at the Salon d'Automne is devoted to his work. This is his year of triumph.

1904 Renoir Retrospective Exhibition at the Salon d'Automne. Picasso settles for good in Paris, at the "Bateau Lavoir."

1905 Cézanne exhibits again at the Salon d'Automne and again at the Indépendants. Leaves off work on the "Grandes Baigneuses" on which he had been toiling for seven years .

1905 Beginning of Picasso's Rose Period; he now meets Apollinaire. Struck down with arthritis, Renoir settles for good at Cagnes. Seurat and Van Gogh exhibitions at the Indépendants. Derain joins Matisse at Collioure, where the latter paints "Luxe, calme et volupté." The Fauves at the Salon d'Automne.

1906 On October 15, caught in a rainstorm while at work in the open country on his "Cabanon de Jourdan," Cézanne collapsed on the roadside. A passing laundry cart picked him up and he was carried home. He died on October 22.

1906 Picasso begins work on "Les Demoiselles d'Avignon" and meets Matisse and Derain. The Douanier Rousseau meets Apollinaire, Delaunay and Picasso. Gauguin exhibition at the Salon d'Automne. Juan Gris arrives in Paris.

SELF-PORTRAIT, C. 1877. (24 × 18½″)
THE PHILLIPS COLLECTION, WASHINGTON.

PORTRAIT OF CÉZANNE

Taken in his twentieth year, the earliest photograph we have of Cézanne, from which he awkwardly, naïvely painted his first self-portrait, perhaps his very first picture, shows a dark, moody young man looking for all the world like a carbonaro about to sell his life dearly or to pit his forces against lurking, indefinable dangers. Of old French stock, the son of a hatmaker in a small, provincial town of southern France, Cézanne, we may take it, was something of a problem-child from the very start: high-strung, quarrelsome, stubborn, hot-headed and shy all at once, but withal a serious, hard-working boy. At school nothing left him indifferent; he applied himself to his lessons and took prizes in Greek, Latin, the sciences, and everything in fact except drawing. He was consumed with a desire to master every subject, a youthful trait of many painters, common to all periods of art history: the passionate desire to embrace and understand everything, but always unmethodically and with a certain flightiness, impelled more by intellectual curiosity than by any real interest in specific objects or fields of study—and always, too, with a vague yearning for escape from the dreary side of life, from oneself most of all. Sometimes, of course, these restless aspirations conceal a deep-seated need to expose and correct the defects of the world; in another sense they are the obscure inner forces that stir within every great artist and prompt him to recast the world in his own image. But Cézanne for the time being—round about 1852, in which year he entered the Collège Bourbon at Aix-en-Provence—was still a raw youth toiling at his lessons, for nothing ever came easy to him. On the side, as might be expected, he wrote small poems. He had a good ear for music, showing a particular fondness for the barrel-organ, warbled a song in his idle moments, and played the cornet in the school band. He must have been sincerely attached to his instrument, since we find it hanging on the wall behind a still life he painted many years later (Goldschmidt Collection, New York). Most important of all, he showed a keen interest in the plastic and pictorial arts. He took to drawing even as a child, and from his tenth year on, at the Pensionnat Saint-Joseph, a Spanish monk is said to have taken a fancy to the boy and trained his hand. At expansive moments in the company of Zola, his boyhood companion who even then urged him to paint seriously and become an artist, the names of Rembrandt, Veronese and Rubens rose continually to his lips. He confided his dreams to his mother and she affectionately observed that he, too, like Rubens and Veronese, bore the name of Paul. It is true that into these enthusiasms crept little discernment; Corot, Courbet, Gérome, Meissonier, all were mingled indiscriminately in his esteem. Restless and active as he was, keen on discovering things for himself, young Cézanne came like a complete innocent upon the methods and techniques of the artists of his day and their forerunners; true to his nature, he reacted to them almost like an unschooled bungler, but a bungler with flashes of genius. He was always to work in this way, inflicting disorder on the well-ordered models before him and violating the tried-and-proved methods he was expected to assimilate. Nothing would deter him; he insisted on learning for himself.

But his mental life, intense and turbulent though it was, failed to work off all his energies and went hand in hand with an almost feverish physical activity. A passionate mountain-climber, he tackled one by one the most difficult peaks in the pre-alpine region around Aix. He was a powerful swimmer, hunted in and out of season, and we may take it for granted that, for this young man, playing the cornet came down to a form of much-needed physical rather than musical exercise. His schoolfellows must have found him very hard to get on with.

Firm-set in his opinions, incapable of modifying his views or conceding a point, he simply avoided people who differed or seemed likely to differ with him. All his faculties incited him to conceive and aspire on the grand scale, and he was refused admittance to the Ecole des Beaux-Arts in Paris, probably quite rightly, the professors who examined the work he submitted adding the mention: "He over-paints." For all his prizes at school, he advanced too slowly for us to believe that he was a brilliant rather than merely a diligent student. Sheer tenacity saw him through his "baccalauréat," which even so he took rather late, at the age of nineteen. Thereupon, at the instance of his father, who would hear of no other course of study, he enrolled in the law school at Aix. But he loathed the subject from the bottom of his heart and stuck to it only long enough to come up with the idea of setting the whole French code of laws to verse, much as the valet in Molière had dreamt of turning Roman history into a long string of madrigals.

Under the mask of his gruff nature and (very often) overbearing manner, Cézanne was all his life chronically, congenitally timid and shrinking. He stood so much in fear of his father's wrath—which seems never to have burst out, for all in all he was not an obdurate man—that for years his liaison with Hortense Fiquet was a secret to no one but to Cézanne *père*. His mother was the only person in whom he confided, and in various matters she saw to it that paternal decrees were amended or annulled to suit her son's inclinations. In this way Cézanne overcame his father's opposition to the career he fancied for himself, that of an artist. But in time his timidity came to border on an almost morbid state; he could tolerate no one's watching him while he worked and shrunk from physical contact. Cézanne was a sea of dark, stormy forces, a mountain of obstinacy, yet he could never face up to the things and people around him. "Isolation is all I'm good for," he said. "Then at least no one will get his hooks into me... Weak in life as I am, I think it best to put my faith in Rome." And so he did, practicing Catholicism with sufficient fervor for his friends to regard him as something of a bigot. He looked up to those who impressed him as strong personalities, and for years stood in admiration of Zola, valued his opinions and meekly took his advice; but when in the end he felt that Zola had let him down, he described him as "a vile friend and a mediocre mind."

Into his need to expend pent-up physical forces we may read an outward sign of his deeply sensual nature. But his fear of women went equally deep; their very specific charms, so mysterious a quantity for him, troubled and intimidated him. As a rule he avoided painting from the nude model, and the reason of course lay in his timidity and inhibitions rather than any fear of what the gossiping tongues of a provincial town might say. He painted an *Orgy*, but his own intimacies were few and his love-life insignificant. Instead of seeking their company, he merely dreamt of women and in his youth found some satisfaction in composing elegiacal poems in their honor, some of which were frankly indecent. But the feminine element inspired a kind of dread and repugnance in him which he never overcame.

Essentially a self-taught artist, he seems from the outset to have carried over something of this originality into his mental and moral make-up, whose features owed little or nothing to his mother and father. Out of the depths of his inexplicable originality came an unprecedented vision of what painting might be, and with it the invention of unprecedented technical means. These, mysteriously compounded with his genius, produced the disconcerting antithesis of spontaneous, "illogical" promptings and almost painful restraint that stood behind his achievement, whose finest tribute came, perhaps unwittingly, from the ever cautious, ever reticent Maurice Denis when he spoke of the "absurd and splendid works" of the old master of Aix.

BACK TO VERONESE AND DELACROIX

CÉZANNE was much too headstrong and proud a young man to yield fully to any influence from outside. Strange to say, the great influence of his life was to be his own work as, gathering power slowly, it accumulated behind him and took specific form in his eyes. But in the sixties he poignantly felt the need to lean on somebody or something.

Even at this stage he banked on color as the form of expression that best sorted with his temperament. Thus it was only natural that his admiration should go to the Venetians, who, carried away by their oriental dreams and memories of Byzantium, showed no concern for the accepted facts of history. In Veronese in particular he found the voluptuous color-masses he loved, a luminous atmosphere and spacious architecture.

But a more immediate confirmation of his likes came with his discovery of Delacroix, a man of his own century whose work, in many ways the sole precedent of his boldest dreams, encouraged both his "romantic" flair and his growing sense of discipline. After *The Orgy* it took him no less than ten years to control his highflown romantic fancy. Only then, as he meditated the example of Delacroix—who for all his irrepressible exaltation preferred Racine to Victor Hugo—did he realize how much imagination owed to the steady guidance of well-mastered technical procedures. From him Cézanne learnt the extent to which the secrets of symmetry, formal relationships and proportions can lend an abiding and graceful solidity to the painter's inspirations. And without doing violence to the revolutionary promptings of his instinct, he learnt to put these to constructive ends in keepings with the over-all vision that shaped his work, in which, finally, instinct and reason may truly be said to stand in balance, thanks to the most highly developed expression of color that any painter has given us.

18

A comparison of these two works reveals at a glance the distance Cézanne had covered in the space of a decade. The spectacular sensuality and eroticism of his *Orgy* have given way in the *Bacchanal* to the pleasure of handling forms for their own sake, while the color-masses, instead of running wild, serve the best interests of the composition as a whole. His *Orgy* was an eruption of powerful brushwork; the *Bacchanal* is a harmony of rhythms promising all the architectural solidity to come.

BACCHANAL (LA LUTTE D'AMOUR), 1875-1876. (16½ × 21½″)
PRIVATE COLLECTION, PARIS.

THE ORGY, 1864-1868. (51 × 31¾″) PRIVATE COLLECTION, PARIS.

As is plain to see from *The Orgy*, Cézanne owed a considerable debt to Veronese, of whom he said: "He painted as the eye sees, with no more effort than an accomplished dancer." Discovering Delacroix he wrote: "He was the first to paint in volumes since the Old Masters, but there is a fever in his work that is lacking in theirs." Cézanne made his own version of Delacroix's *Medea*, superbly intensifying its dynamism.

MEDEA (AFTER DELACROIX), 1879-1882. (15 × 9¾″)
WATERCOLOR, KUNSTHAUS, ZURICH.

THE ROMANTIC PERIOD

CÉZANNE'S career as an artist got off to a start that seemed anything but promising when he won a very modest prize in drawing at an art academy in Aix in 1858. Thoroughgoing romantic though he was soon to be, for the moment he kept his ambitions to himself, working hard on his own and following the lines suggested to him by his innate sense of order and construction. His father had advanced from hatter to banker, his business prospered, and in 1859 he bought a large country-house on the outskirts of Aix: Le Jas de Bouffan. Here Cézanne fitted up a studio for himself and proceeded to cover the walls of the house with large decorative panels—insipid productions, which he signed "Ingres"—and copies from artists he admired, amongst them Lancret's *Hide and Seek*. No one took him seriously and his father indulgently let him work this eccentricity out of his system. Cézanne was not precocious. He had seen the canvases in the Aix Museum, which at that time could boast little more than second-rate followers of Caravaggio, whose style was still a closed book to him, and conventional works by contemporary academicians; he had yet to receive the psychic "shock" that would open his eyes. At Aix he moved in a group of local artists, Emperaire, Solari, Loubon, none of whom had anything to teach him. Zola was a stimulating companion; they read poems together, admiring Victor Hugo, Lamartine and Alfred de Musset. But it was the impassioned romanticism of their poetry that appealed to him rather than the profoundly human message it contains, which went by him completely.

About the time he was twenty-five, however, a change came over Cézanne as the struggle began in earnest between his animal sensuality and his timid attempts at self-expression. He had until now only dabbled in brushes and paints, but with

THE MAN IN A BLUE CAP, 1865-1867. (31⅜ × 25¼″)
METROPOLITAN MUSEUM OF ART, NEW YORK.

his first trip to Paris in 1861 painting became the guiding passion of his life. Encouraged by Zola and having wrung reluctant permission from his father, who insisted on accompanying him to Paris, he stood for the entrance examinations at the Ecole des Beaux-Arts, but failed to pass. He fell back on the Académie Suisse, where he met Guillaumin and, most important of all, Pissarro, whose influence on him was salutary and decisive. He eagerly visited the Louvre, where he could revel in genuine works by Caravaggio, by Velazquez, Rembrandt and Rubens. He was won over at once by what he saw of Courbet and Delacroix, and soon fell in with a whole set of younger painters— Renoir, Manet, Sisley, Monet, in addition to Pissarro—whose advanced outlook and self-assurance surprised, excited and encouraged him all at once. The Impressionists-to-be also opened his eyes to nature, which at Aix had been little more than the necessary background for his hunting trips and his climbs in the mountains. He painted with new hope and confidence, working on in so characteristic a way that it has been said of Cézanne that he did not paint because he was an artist, but became an artist by dint of painting—two very different things. At no time was his development the outcrop of unexpected discoveries and spontaneous innovations. He hammered out his genius on the forge of hard work; he willed his progress and deliberated in advance on the course it should take, a frame of mind reflected in his increasing need for architectural order and structural solidity. Cézanne never painted "as a bird sings," as did Monet and his friends; he struggled through intermittent fits of discouragement and despair, some of them melodramatic and long-lived, such as the Impressionists never experienced. But he always broke into the clear again and, gaining confidence, slowly rid himself of inhibitions of which he had hardly been aware, much as now, alongside the almost gloating sensuality we find in his compositions of nudes, his romantic style rose to a note genuinely expressive of the pure joy of the paints, while at the same period he produced an initial series of fine still lifes, landscapes and portraits, well composed works full of conviction and sobriety.

For the first time he let himself go in an attempt to work off some of the lusty animal spirits within him. And the Cézanne who had pinned on the wall of his studio a reproduction of Couture's insipidly conventional *Roman Orgy* had soon produced an *Orgy* of his own, a volcanic eruption of forms and feelings, which we reproduce in the opening pages of this book.

This work brought home to him one of the peculiar functions of Romanticism, namely that of channeling and releasing the artist's pent-up feelings. It made him forget his timidity, his gropings, the want of self-confidence that might have led him either to practice a sickly-sweet, sentimental brand of painting, such as he had mused on with Zola, or, in deference to his faith, to restrict himself to religious art. But nothing of the kind happened. On the contrary, he set vigorously about unleashing his sensuality under cover of a naturally violent temper. In the letters he wrote we see him blustering, roaring like a lion, and using coarse language freely and fluently. His choice of subjects and the titles he gave them prove the intensity of his feelings, and we have, together with *The Orgy*, *The Rape*, *The Temptation of St Anthony*, *The Murder*, *The Woman Strangled*, and many others.

The soft-stepping, religious-minded Cézanne of a few years before threw caution to the winds. Slow stirrings of genius threatened to become a paroxysm as he saw what he could do with colors and forms—deep colors and lusty forms that frequently echoed the masters he most admired. Then his sensuality took a turn towards sublimation, welling up in forms overlaid with heavy-textured pigment that is often like a foretaste of Van Gogh, though stabler on the whole, with none of

MELTING SNOW AT L'ESTAQUE, 1870. (28¾ × 36¼″)
WILDENSTEIN COLLECTION, NEW YORK.

During his romantic period Cézanne was inclined to look at nature more from an outright dynamic angle than from any other, and dealt in systems of forms that were eye-catching rather than rigorously ordered. When he painted a landscape, storms were always brewing on the horizon, skies were always lowering above. He had no eye yet for the deeper side of nature and continued for some time to paint her superficially in terms of imposing patches of contrasting color, for which he drew inspiration from the Spanish and Italian *tenebrosi*. He spattered his colors across the canvas in broad, disheveled touches agleam with crude highlights.

In the figure of the tall, slightly stooping woman and the bending tree-trunk at the right we have a notable early example of those rhythmic repetitions, re-echoings of forms, that Cézanne was later to incorporate in so many pictures. The tree strikes a somber note into a sky that, though touched up with picturesque accents of color, still casts the shadow of a threat over this uneasy gathering. The lay-out of the figures remains rather rudimentary: four solemn picnickers a dog and a disdainful onlooker, all turning an anxious gaze on the outspread cloth and its frugal luncheon —two shining red apples throwing a murky shadow that betrays as yet none of the colorful shadow-play made so much of by the Impressionists.

THE LUNCHEON ON THE GRASS, 1869-1870. (23 ½ × 31 ¾″)
PRIVATE COLLECTION, PARIS.

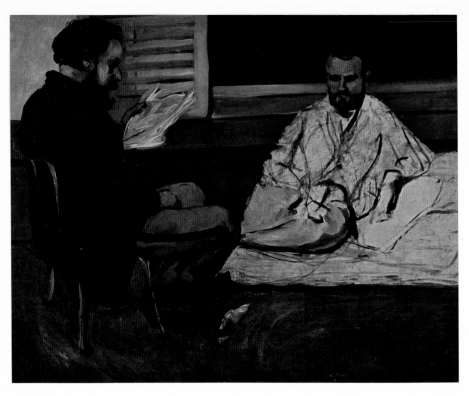

PAUL ALEXIS READING TO ZOLA, 1869-1870. (51½×63¼″)
WILDENSTEIN COLLECTION, NEW YORK.

In the initial works of his romantic period Cézanne's inspiration came
chiefly from the Venetians, the Spaniards, even from the prints in fashion
magazines that happened to fall into his hands. But here we see the impact
of his contemporaries on his style. Following on the influence of Delacroix
and Courbet, obviously it was Manet who led him to give over his decorative extravaganzas and his congested impasto in favor of quiet interiors.

PORTRAIT OF LOUIS-AUGUSTE CÉZANNE, THE ARTIST'S FATHER, 1866-1867. ▶
(78½×47¼″) PRIVATE COLLECTION, PARIS

the Dutchman's overwrought brushwork. For the libido of the man never quite succeeded in upsetting the balance of the artist. Let there be no mistake: all these early works are, at bottom, struggles with form and not with the flesh, disciplined as they obviously are by the countryman's sound good sense and the wholesome effects of a solid classical education. Cézanne could not foresee, of course, that the day was almost at hand when he would cry out against the "contours that melt away" and take vigorous steps to fix them firmly. For the time being he vented his feelings with a vengeance, often helpless to impose order and architecture on them. Intent on saying what he had to say, he had no time to haggle over the means of expression. He seized on whatever surged up within him and improvised bravura pieces along the lines of those he so much admired by Courbet and Delacroix. But they show more carrying power than staying power; textural vigor takes the place of drawing and linework, and even that rings a little hollow, despite a thick impasto slapped on with the palette-knife, as in *The Man in a Blue Cap*. He worked recklessly ahead in this vein, almost blindly, it would seem, with the result that his romantic compositions sprang vividly to life in an upsurge of poetry and sinewed strength. He whipped into shape a variety of voluptuous, well-rounded forms that arch up and swell out on all sides—clouds, haunches, breasts, undulating countrysides and so on. But for all its throbbing life, for all its intense warmth and authenticity, this dynamism is essentially ingenuous in its torrential force, at times recalling certain works of the Douanier Rousseau. Certainly Cézanne learnt a lot from Michelangelo and Tintoretto, but at no time did he yield to the emasculating influence of the Ecole des Beaux-Arts, rescued no

THE MAN WITH A STRAW HAT (PORTRAIT OF BOYER), 1870-1871. ►
(21⅝ × 15⅜") METROPOLITAN MUSEUM OF ART, NEW YORK.

doubt by the irrepressible vigor and health of his native genius, for he himself was capable of innocently citing Bouguereau and Rubens in the same breath.

Though paying tribute in early works to anecdote and subject-matter, Cézanne gradually conferred on the picture an autonomy whose characteristics he was one of the first to establish. An early example is his very curious *Temptation of St Anthony* (1867-1869), a magnificent piece of work in its own right, but particularly interesting for the way the saint is blandly relegated to the far background, where he almost passes unnoticed, while staged well in the foreground, for the benefit of eye and senses, is a brilliant display of female nudity—all this much in the manner of El Greco's *Martyrdom of St Maurice*, in which the actual episode of the saint's execution occupies but an insignificant corner of the composition, the major part being devoted to a group of distinguished gentlemen who, showing no interest in the fate of the saint, seem to be casually discussing an entirely different matter. The subject itself, then, held less and less appeal for Cézanne. And though obviously *The Temptation of St Anthony* is in the main expressive of his sensual nature, this force had soon lost its grip on him, while the direction in which the picture pointed, aesthetically speaking, continued to hold good. Though his imagination may have seemed a little erratic in its workings as he tested its powers, the ultimate issue was never in doubt. However contradictory in appearance, his aspirations were always the deep reflection of some facet of his temperament, and were not the mere spawn of influences that might have come his way from painter friends of his at Aix whose southern temperaments were superficially akin to his own. Luckily, too, he fell under no persuasion for long, and learnt chiefly from the example of the masters. He was not slow to rid himself of means taken over from his elders, whose recipes and mannerisms had been largely foisted

Here, boldly tackling the most difficult problems of form, Cézanne brought off what is nothing less than a masterpiece. Though he still made play with contrasts of black and white tempered with a wide range of intermediate tones, fairly high in the scale, much as he had done in his *Luncheon on the Grass*, now for the first time he ordered a still life composition with a full sense of what architecture means, building it on a solid masonry of verticals and horizontals, and fitting these into an organized disorder that capitalizes to the utmost on the rhythmic possibilities of form and structure for which the objects here might have been deliberately chosen.

THE BLACK CLOCK, 1869-1870. (21 ¼ × 28 ¾″). NIARCHOS COLLECTION.

A MODERN OLYMPIA, 1872-1873. ($18 \times 21\frac{1}{2}''$)
DR PAUL GACHET BEQUEST, LOUVRE, PARIS.

Cézanne seldom bothered to date his pictures, so that any attempt to fix their exact chronology is largely a matter of guesswork. The dating of this work is fairly reliable, however, as he painted it while staying at Dr Gachet's home at Auvers, where he is known to have been a frequent guest round about 1872-1873. Probably he had had the subject in mind for some time; in any case, this fresh outburst of exuberant brushwork harks back to his romantic fling of the sixties, though somewhat steadied now by the sober example of Manet's great picture on the same theme.

VASE WITH FLOWERS, 1873-1875. (16⅛ × 10⅝″)
DR PAUL GACHET BEQUEST, LOUVRE, PARIS.

on him by Gibert, an academic painter whose coaching he was only too happy to have in the early days at Aix, before he had yet turned twenty.

We see him coming into his own as early as 1866—with *The Orgy* still on the stocks, that is—when he produced his *Portrait of the Negro Scipion*, one of the most popular models at the Académie Suisse. In this rugged, almost static work we can detect all the structural architecture that lay ahead, as well as the discipline and freedom united that were soon to form the backbone of Cézanne's aesthetic. In other canvases, too, such as *Paul Alexis reading to Zola, The Man in the Straw Hat* and *The Black Clock*, all reproduced here, the emphasis had decisively shifted from a vein of sensuality to one of pure artistic sensibility, however sensual-minded he remained. No doubt he looked long at Manet and the Spaniards, but the fact of his having taken a leaf or two from their book—notably an increasing fondness for those antitheses of color that led him to maintain that, in the end, everything comes down to color contrasts—is further evidence of his new and intense concern for the purely technical problems he had not yet seriously tackled. Thus he made his way towards a new architecture, exclusively pictorial, whose rudiments he discerned both in the Old Masters and in the work of his impressionist friends.

If other great names have been coupled with his—those of Veronese, Tintoretto and Caravaggio, for instance, as well as Courbet, Daumier and Delacroix—it is only fair to add that his art arose on an aesthetic basis which, however hard to define at this stage, had perhaps never been dreamt of by these masters. Neither the fine decorative flair of the three Italians nor the romantic trend of his three great countrymen deflected Cézanne in his intuitive advance towards *pure painting*—i.e. painting for its own sake, if you will, a notion whose repercussions on all modern art have been so deep and far-reaching.

CÉZANNE AND IMPRESSIONISM

CÉZANNE left Aix for Paris many times, but his dislike of city life was so deep-seated that he never stayed long, and even then continually changed studios. He met the Impressionists in Paris and saw them whenever he was there, either at the Café Guerbois, or at nearby Pontoise, La Roche-Guyon and above all Auvers. He was drawn at once to the new art they were practicing and learnt much from their company. But we shall see in a moment why, in actual fact, after having won him over, they exerted so little influence on the deep trend of his own ideas about the art of painting.

Out of all these early contacts, however, one thing becomes quite clear: to the Impressionists goes the credit for opening Cézanne's eyes to nature. Needless to say, he had long since advanced beyond the naïvely conventional landscapes of the years 1858-1860, lost interest in copying the masters, and sought inspiration elsewhere than in fashion prints culled from such magazines as the *Musée des Familles* and the *Illustrateur des Dames*. But till he came back from Paris he had never really seen Provence; now he looked upon its rural beauties with new eyes, and new emotions stirred within him. The Impressionists no doubt passed on to him many a trick of the trade. Yet when all was said and done his congenital sense of caution and independence kept him from embracing the new aesthetic unreservedly. Incurably stand-offish, he preferred not to stray from the narrow path which he obscurely felt to be his own. Ratiocinator that he was, he wondered that the Impressionists could so casually go their way without niggling over their exact aims and the eventual consequences. He reproached them for failing to give the mind its due. "Monet is only an eye" was his comment. For him "the eye is trained" by nature, but he saw no reason for nature's becoming the painter's exclusive object of passion. He saw her not as a source of impressions and sensations, but as an incentive to organize the picture—Cézanne's consuming ambition.

What did he gain from Impressionism then? First of all, step by step, he outgrew the tumultuous allegories, more or less mythological in character, in which the female nude had played the leading role; these he had been led to paint by the dictates of his temperament, his classical schooling, his study of the masters and the urgings of Zola. Next came what was certainly a vital factor in his development: the discovery of nature, as seen through the eyes of the Impressionists. But he was not long in looking at nature from a specifically impressionist angle; soon he saw her with his own eyes, and never as an end in herself but only as a means to something else. Diffidently at first he modified his palette. The old violence subsided, and with it the old, ill-considered tossings of color, as he advanced towards a new conception of color, simpler, wider in range, much more refined. Until now, as we have noted, he had modeled forms in the Bolognese and Spanish manners, striking heroic, often dissonant contrasts of browns and blacks against lighter tones and white. Taking his cue from the Impressionists he put his colors directly on the canvas without bothering about a ground-sketch, accepting the principle that there are no lines in nature, only contrasts. Now, too, for the first time, he timidly set up his easel in the open air. Taken in hand by Pissarro, he turned out a few landscapes in the park at Issy-les-Moulineaux, on the outskirts of Paris. But for the moment nature seemed to him almost flat and insipid, and so she continued to seem as long as he stood before her passively —until the day, that is, when screwing up his courage he completely recast what he saw to suit the painter in him.

But the Cézanne of this period had only begun to cement his relations with nature, and we shall see later how he got on

DR GACHET'S HOUSE AT AUVERS, 1872-1873. (26×21⅝″)
COLLECTION OF MR AND MRS WILLIAM GOETZ,
LOS ANGELES, CALIFORNIA.

Perhaps the great thing the Impressionists passed on to Cézanne was something of their insight into nature. Now he scrutinized her with loving care before putting a stroke on his canvas. As he got into the habit of working in the fields and countryside, he discarded the blacks of his early days and began to revel in vivid dabs of paint, though he still showed no inclination to practice either separate-stroke brushwork or the systematic juxtaposition of tones. A curious geometrical device, however, is resorted to in this panoramic *View of Auvers*: the profusion of pointed roofs, like so many jagged sawteeth prickling across the canvas.

VIEW OF AUVERS, 1873-1875. (25 ½ × 31 ½″)
ART INSTITUTE, CHICAGO.

THE HERMITAGE, PONTOISE, 1875-1877. (14¼ × 21⅛″)
STAEDTISCHES MUSEUM, WUPPERTAL.

Cézanne's brooding concern with geometry comes into the open again in
this landscape whose backbone, so to speak, is identical to that of the
Black Clock: a vertical rising slightly to the right of center, linked by a
sturdy mid-picture horizontal to a corresponding vertical that runs down
slightly to the left of center. It was Pissarro who urged Cézanne to paint
from nature. Carried away by his initial enthusiasm, he felt no qualms
about tackling the immense panorama of Auvers reproduced on the opposite page. Here, however, the wiser perhaps for a few years' experience,
he concentrated on a motif much more limited in compass.

Cézanne took obvious pleasure in extending the variety of his tones and stepping up blues, yellows, greens and reds to a rich and sonorous pitch. But all the while he remained on strictly classical ground, with classical models uppermost in his mind. During his stays in Paris he was an assiduous visitor to the Louvre, where he came to know and admire Chardin —"a wily old boy who knew every trick of the trade," as he called him. His inspiration for the canvas below obviously derives from the fluteglass and knife that run like a leitmotiv through Chardin's still lifes.

A DESSERT, 1873-1877. (23¼ × 28¾")
CARROLL S. TYSON COLLECTION, PHILADELPHIA.

with her. As it was, he made great strides in the "training of his eye" round about 1871-1872, gaining considerable confidence and experience in treating landscape motifs which, as Courbet had strenuously advised, he chose completely at random. But apparently falling prey to momentary doubts and misgivings, he reverted several times to his earlier romantic manner, which he must have abandoned with some reluctance. Examples of this step backward are his *Modern Olympia* and *Afternoon at Naples*, subjects handled in much the same way as his early *Autopsy* (1867) and *The Temptation of St Anthony* (1867). But the old technique of his romantic pictures had lost its piquant spontaneity, its high-handed driving force. Now it seemed simply feverish, mere excitation rather than dynamism; his extravagances no longer carried the deep, sensual conviction of earlier days.

The truth is that his state of mind was gravely troubled as he came to taste the indifference, not to say hostility of the public, on the one hand, and the lashing strictures of the critics on the other. Instead of taking heart from the sincere (if measured) encouragement given him by a few clairvoyant men, he lapsed into gloominess at the diatribes of those who sneered at his work. One critic, though he had had a good word for Monet, Renoir and Pissarro, did not scruple to write: "Cézanne now stands out as no more than a poor deluded madman who paints in fits of delirium tremens." His work was rejected at the official Salon with clocklike regularity, while one day at the Ecole des Beaux-Arts a rowdy crowd of students got hold of one of his canvases and paraded it about amid jeering and cat-calls. The cup overflowed when he chanced to read Balzac's *Le chef-d'œuvre inconnu*. He read his own fate into that of Frenhofer, the painter whose genius lay in the very futility of his efforts, and put the book down in despair. No wonder then that he seized at the straw when Pissarro, wise and kindly as

THE BUFFET, 1873-1877. (29½ × 31¾")
MUSEUM OF FINE ARTS, BUDAPEST.

Showing no sign of deviation from pure geometry, Cézanne's experiments were woven round more or less obvious figures—circles, ovals and cones—and fed on such biscuits as these, which with their plate were an ideal pretext for a quilt-work of parallelopipeds. In defiance of the curves it ought to yield, the bunched-up tablecloth produces a criss-cross of angles and triangles that rise up and tower protectively over the big red apple in the foreground. Cézanne's poetic flair, however, on its guard against overcrowding, led him to space out objects with a very free hand.

usual, advised him to work seriously out-of-doors. He may have seemed to act on this suggestion half-heartedly, but the results are there. His palette brightened up considerably; his brushwork grew lighter, defter. He gave up the stodgy impasto of his romantic period and adopted the classical, right-to-left brushstroke. Ridding his palette of ochres, blacks and earthy colors, he began to dabble in the seven colors of the prism. Foregoing the outright modeling of his previous compositions, he investigated the secrets of the famous divided brushstrokes and rhythmic hatchings. But careful never to let himself be swept off his feet by his impressions, he brushed in the picture cautiously, thoughtfully, never with bravura. Unlike his friends, out-and-out Impressionists, he made no attempt to express the objective sensations of the eye as they impinged on the retina, but composed with them, refined them, weeded them out as it were. He did not revel in discoveries whose consequences he could not foresee, as Monet was wont to do. Something of the peasant kept him on his guard, made him a thrifty user of the resources he was hoarding up. Most of all he dreaded shallowness and fragility, and anything that smacked of rashness or hazardous enterprise.

Yet this was the man who was soon to revolutionize the art of painting. He was, however, in no hurry to do so and measured his steps, not capitalizing on his impressions as such. His instinct warned him against representing merely that aspect of the object that fills the eye. He was the more wary of outward appearances as he was now initiating himself into the arcana of color, the workings of the complementaries in particular. Following the Impressionists in this, he went so far as to rid his canvas of local tones, but only provisionally. And when he came back to them, as he soon did, he could hardly bring himself to dissolve the object in a light-drenched atmosphere rendered in small, scattered touches which, in his

eyes, were far too arbitrarily broken up, divided off and juxtaposed. Already he was obsessed with the problem of securing his contour-lines, which preoccupied him for so long. By this time, too, of course, he had come to prize the light whose virtues he had been ignorant of only shortly before, when he still worked in terms of conventional lighting and melodramatic contrasts. Cézanne saw that the true light of day breaks down and modifies tones and shades, gives wonderful scope for the modulations of color in which he was soon to excel, and is the deciding factor in choosing local tones, to which, after trying to do without them, he reverted for good. For him, however, the great thing about light was its texture-revealing properties. And he used it in this way, rather than merely to illuminate the object superficially, for if he retained one thing from his youthful gropings as a painter, this was his fondness for full-bodied volumes and unbridled arabesques. In his hands colors never ran riot, never burst out in splashing fountains of light; on the contrary, they were magnificent timber to him, with which he built up the object in a picture-space of his own devising, instead of drowning it out in a limitless atmospheric haze that did no more than produce an "impression" and suggest vague "ideas" no one could put his finger on. This was his first decisive step towards becoming what he was destined to be: the pioneer of pure painting. Unlike Monet, Cézanne, even at this early stage, saw to it that his color never got out of hand, never crowded out form, but signified it, defined it in all its density, and strictly in terms of the picture dimensions, though without ever falling back on such all too obvious tactile values as those implied by the simple transposition of visual impressions on to the canvas.

◀ PORTRAIT OF VICTOR CHOCQUET, 1876-1877. (18⅛ × 14⅛″)
COLLECTION OF LORD VICTOR ROTHSCHILD, CAMBRIDGE, ENGLAND.

What was his opposition to Impressionism but his refusal to sacrifice form on the altar of color? Luckily for him he was so naturally, so nobly gifted a colorist that he felt no need to proclaim, as one of his friends had done, that without it no hope of salvation remained. So he turned his attention to filling what he considered to be the chinks in his painter's armor. It never occurred to him, when he bewailed his inability to get the contours he wanted, that by defining them too sharply, too precisely, he might only succeed in repressing form, stunting its growth, as did the academic painters whose work, none the less, roused his envy. The fact is that he was not quite musician enough to ask of painting that it should transform tangible reality into a far-flung, unreal, abstract space, totally timeless. Which, to his mind, is what Impressionism did to a large extent, vying with music in its dynamism and, like music, never fixing the contours of things but lurking in the shadow of the real world. In this respect it took all the genius of Monet to brave the risks involved—and they are still being braved today, though from another angle, by abstract art.

After he had abundantly tested out its possibilities, these were the considerations that led Cézanne, along with Manet, Degas and Renoir, to become one of the staunchest adversaries of the Impressionist way of seeing. Doggedly pursuing his own version of the "truth," he saw nothing of any use or promise to him in procedures that staked their claim on appearances rather than on a reality which, if it could not be embraced, could at least be approached and felt out. Though Cézanne never regarded nature as a corpse to be dissected, his own sense of order aspired to her order, and led to the synthesis he at last effected between the "thrill" nature touched off in his sensibility and the fermenting action of his creative faculties, which seized on it and developed it with logical rigor and imaginative power.

MADAME CÉZANNE IN A RED EASYCHAIR, C. 1877. (28 ½ × 22″)
MUSEUM OF FINE ARTS, BOSTON.

THE CONSTRUCTIVE PERIOD: ANALYSIS

IF in his romantic period Cézanne remained in the thrall of traditional influences, and while flirting with Impressionism showed a certain docility towards his friends, who already knew what they wanted, the reason is simply that he had yet to find himself entirely. Developing slowly, but with relentless steadiness, he instinctively followed the good counsel of the best teachers: learn everything you can and absorb whatever part of it comes natural to you. In other words, instead of sticking to the letter of what he learnt, he drew sustenance from the spirit behind it all. Demanding crystal clarity at all costs, he brought his analytic faculties to bear on the workings of his own inspiration, not without stumblings and false alarms, it is true, for the way he had chosen to go was a completely new one. He was called upon to shift for himself, to invent new means as he went along, though these rarely satisfied him at once and came in for reiterated elaboration, carried on year in, year out. In a sense, each day's work became a stubborn effort to wipe the slate clean, to free his hand of the conventional practices all young artists are indoctrinated with. Surely it is not going too far to regard Cézanne as a kind of inveterate primitive, not to say eccentric, but an eccentric whose genius justified his own description of himself: "the Primitive of the path I have opened up." Which is another way of saying that he re-invented the art of painting by going back to its original sources. Between the art-forms that have shaped painting since the Renaissance and those created by Cézanne lies a gulf that can only be described as a fundamental difference of kind.

What was the nature of Cézanne's innovation? It was nothing more nor less than a radically new approach to the essential problems of painting, restated in terms of geometry. Having subsisted since Renaissance times on the age-old notion

THE POOL AT THE JAS DE BOUFFAN, C. 1878. (20⅝ × 22″)
PRIVATE COLLECTION, PARIS.

The researches of his analytic period were curiously embodied in a trend towards a stiff, almost ungainly simplification. The composition takes form within a kind of geometrical continuum that leaves no room for the random or fanciful. Houses are bare and forbidding, trees stark and leafless; the soft curves of the romantic period are no more to be found, only straight lines and angles. Subordinating all else to architectonic equilibrium, he took strange liberties with verisimilitude: the tree growing at the very edge of the water and the completely arbitrary reflections, the whole stretch of land between the pool and the house beyond not even being reflected at all.

Cézanne never made the picture more autonomous and absolute than when working in watercolors. While he went the limit in this direction at the end of his life, even in this middle period he cultivated the watercolor as a means of working out his oils beforehand and varying them afterwards. These two pictures reflect the transition from his impressionist to his constructive period. The cottage by the stream is almost swept up in a torrent of leafage, while the white ground of the paper produces patches of luminosity. In the *Château de Médan*, a theme he took over for an oil-painting only slightly later, the lay-out in terms of verticals and horizontals is noticeably more rigorous and the colors are more daintily brushed in.

LANDSCAPE IN PROVENCE, 1875-1878. ($12\frac{1}{2} \times 18''$) WATERCOLOR.
KUNSTHAUS, ZURICH.

of nature-imitation, painting now stood fair to revive all that
was oldest and fundamental in the art—painting as it had been
before the spirit of scientific experiment had made its claim on
artists, as it had been when the cavemen covered their walls
with graffiti, when the fresco-painters and illuminators were
only imaginative men intent on expressing visions partaking
distinctly of the mind rather than the senses, when, in short,
artists had not yet become the exemplary pupils of one another
whose virtuoso exploits fill the pages of art-history.

A further stage in Cézanne's advance may be noted at this point, for it characterizes both the man and the artist. From the eighties onward, though he had yet to work all the kinks out of it, he had laid the solid, immovable bases of his mature style. One result of this was that he no longer paid any heed to what others were doing. Not only had he lost his interest in their activities, but these had even become suspect and their findings problematical in his eyes, opposed as they were to the lines along which he himself was working. He even went to the opposite extreme of such practices as he had felt no need to adopt, and forced positions that would have made another man think twice, but which he regarded as untenable or outmoded, and wished to show up. Here we have the true Cézanne, the gruff, willful, dictatorial rustic, at bottom far from being so confident in his star, but firm-set on seeming so. Occasionally he seemed to glean something from another artist, but no one was more honest than he and if once or twice he borrowed he never realized it.

Though he never thought of it in this way, Cézanne's ambition differed little from that of every painter: to retrieve the things of childhood that seem to have disappeared for ever. No wonder then that he deliberately hoped to start from scratch. Intuitively he sided with Pascal, who had proposed "to calculate beyond what calculation has hitherto led to." His pride forbade him to impose limits on himself, so that he, "a mere painter," could wax eloquent over "the boundless things of nature that inexorably attract me." Obviously Cézanne saw large and made no secret of it. But it was more than vainglory when he reduced his building materials to the cylinder, cone and sphere; he did so in the most empirical manner, much as peasant builders do when they abide by elementary geometric principles in putting up houses which, if not architecturally perfect, are none the less admirably proportioned.

Whereas the composition of *The Pool at the Jas de Bouffan* took its rise on a schematic ground-plan purely analytic in nature, now, in *The Turn of the Road*, even though much the same sort of ground-plan underlies the work, Cézanne has more warmly responded to the charms of nature. And the man who had "over-painted" before, set to weaving, with the same fine fullness of texture, a sumptuous tapestry of natural elements which, carried away by the eloquence of his own brush, he staggered and superposed along the lines of a purely imaginary perspective.

THE TURN IN THE ROAD, 1879-1882. (23 ½ × 28 ½″)
MUSEUM OF FINE ARTS, BOSTON.

As a child innocently sets himself the task of drawing an object from memory, so Cézanne worked out the intricate, infinitely varied combinations of space, rhythm and color that went to make his pictures, for the truth is that his love of nature was not sentimental enough for him to piece her back together with the objective realism of Corot, for example. His irrepressible ego led him to imagine another world, touching at many points that of the child who has not yet learnt to obey the rules his elders accept without demur. With Cézanne the making of a picture was the natural outcome of a vision so spontaneously original, thrown so luminously on to the dark screen of his mind that he felt rueful at every attempt to improve on it afterwards, cold-bloodedly, since every deviation from it was a kind of violation in his eyes, and a potent enticement to make a fresh start in hopes this time of keeping more closely to the "original" of his vision, or to cast the work aside unfinished, an "unsuccessful realization." Always a vague, almost academic desire to correct and correct again plagued Cézanne, and in fact impelled him to stringent disciplines of procedure. He was not the man to let his genius have its head. No improviser, no virtuoso, he never began a canvas without first having seen it whole in his mind's eye. Once he had embarked on the actual work, it became an obsession with him until at last he brought it off to his satisfaction. He worked in the grip of a visionary synthesis too intimately a part of his artistic make-up for him to analyze its true nature. The world he painted arose on orderly foundations, within an orderly framework, but it was an order that had nothing to do with that of objective reality. It amounted to a pioneer conception of the work of art as a world self-contained and self-sufficient whose measure cannot be taken. So steadily and powerfully did this world of his take shape and grow that in the works of his last years we have a Cézanne possessed, painting in a paroxysmal frame of mind, clutching

DISH AND BOWL WITH FRUIT, 1879-1882. $(16\frac{3}{4} \times 21\frac{1}{4}'')$
NY CARLSBERG GLYPTOTEK, COPENHAGEN.

Having passed the stage of example and demonstration, Cézanne handles
his perspective with new ease and flexibility. What was theory before, with
the necessary abstractions theory entailed, has become concrete expression.
The objects spread out on the table seem to extend their fullness beyond
the table-top, so suavely blending with the flowery patterns of the background that these are like the overhanging grace-notes re-echoing the
color-poetry of the ripe fruit, and bringing to mind, incidentally, a beautiful
line from Mallarmé: *Eternel conflit d'une guirlande avec la même.*

57

at visions whose splendor surpasses verbal description—pictures stark, pure and full-bodied at once, desperate states of beauty no longer identifiable with the particular form or essence of objects, but pure objects in their own right.

Many an artist's work develops as a kind of tug-of-war between his senses and his reasoning mind. With Cézanne, when the latter finally got the upper hand, we can see that his art, true to the headstrong eccentricity of its maker, was never intended to flatter the eye. Cézanne went out of his way to please no one. Even had he attempted to do so, we may well wonder how much success he would have enjoyed. Strange as this may seem, he looked upon the painter's mission as essentially instructive, educational. He asked himself "if art is not a priestly vocation," and all his research-work, all his discoveries made him an ardent neophyte eager to share the truths he had brought to light, to enjoin them on all comers by means of a dialectic as devoid of guile as it was well-intentioned. In Cézanne we find something of those warrior monks of old who, when preaching failed, converted an infidel by braining him with a crucifix—all for his own good of course. Yet he was certainly not immune to intense fits of moodiness and depression, on occasion even expressing fears for the stability and powers of his mind; his letters abound in such allusions. He never came to realize the extent to which he entertained hallucinations, in the full sense of the term. This is to say that his imagination was fed from two sources: the events and concerns of his private life and the creative vision that exalted the artist in him. Instability of a kind was inevitable, paralyzing all action at one moment, spurring him on the next. This accounts for his periodically casting back to the lessons of the Old Masters, driven as he was from time to time to renew his contact with an established order of art from which his inspired hallucinations increasingly set him adrift, so completely in the end that even

SELF-PORTRAIT, 1879-1882. 25 ½ × 20") KUNSTMUSEUM, BERN.

Cézanne's geometric analyses come to a head here in an outbreak of angles, triangles and parallels, while the luminous face stands out against a colossal cylinder rendered with much warmth as he "drew with the brush."

THREE BATHERS, 1879-1882.(19⅝ × 19⅝″)
MUSÉE DE LA VILLE DE PARIS.

This picture was presented to the Musée du Petit-Palais as a gift by
Henri Matisse, who, as a young painter half a century ago, had scraped his
meager savings together in order to buy it. This is but one canvas in a series
of about fifteen, all on the same theme, in which Cézanne developed and
perfected the notion of building with color that was to have so profound
an effect on Matisse. Of all the pictures of bathers this one stands out
for its undercurrent of rhythmic expression, which pulses beneath a veil
of geometrical patterns with a solid and powerful beat exceptional even
for Cézanne, and which he was even to improve on in the *Grandes Baigneuses*.

60

his overweening pride had all it could do to stifle his doubts. It was all very well for him to say that "the sense of one's own strength makes one modest." He apparently felt no such strength, for in another of his letters we find him crowing: "You know as well as I do that there's only one painter in the world: myself."

But these inner conflicts were shouldered into the background by the hard work of this "constructive period," during which he may be said to have hit his stride. Momentarily forgetting himself, it would seem, he discovered the pure and simple joys of painting, and gave the first unmistakable preview of the consummate craftsmanship and technical mastery that he was to achieve. He scrutinized nature more intently than he ever had before and entered on the building of her great counterpart: his own art as we know it today. Standing before her, he recast and reshuffled what he saw, shaping the whole to ends of his own, creating forms that no longer corresponded to those based on the centuries-old principle of nature-imitation.

What happened is that round about 1878 Cézanne began to conceive his landscapes, still lifes, portraits and nudes not in terms of traditional perspective, which had led to the insertion of a third, a spatial dimension into the flat surface of the canvas, but in terms of a purely imaginary perspective whose only precedent we find in the Primitives and in children's drawings. He ceased to lay out the elements of the picture as conventional ways of seeing demanded, but fitted them into an order of patterns inspired by his emotional response to the natural scene he took as his theme; so disposed, these elements set up spatial relationships of their own. One is reminded of Giotto's carefully partitioned world, or the rhythmic contorsions of form in El Greco's compositions. As a rule, Cézanne's pictures were built up round a central core that was simply a daub of paint; this he proceeded to "modulate," as he described the operation, broadening it out with successive strokes and patches of color until the whole canvas stood covered and—above all—balanced. He built up his picture in staggered planes of color superimposed one atop the other perpendicularly, and thus obtained a self-created spatial recession that owed nothing to nature, nor did it hollow out the picture-surface. "I see overlapping planes before me and sometimes lines that seem to fall away," was how he put it. But Cézanne kept his eye on the object steadily and insisted on locating it in the picture-space as he conceived it, which had nothing to do with the haphazard, tricked-up impression of space, created by a partial dismantling of the object, that has since become a stock-in-trade of so many second-rate painter-decorators. He never lost his awe, his fatalistic respect for the virgin surface of the canvas, something perhaps of the apprehension Mallarmé admitted to feeling before the immaculate white of the unwritten page. It was not unusual for him to leave certain parts of the canvas unpainted when he failed to find what he felt was needed to fill them. He regarded the canvas not simply as a material support for his paints, but as a kind of rectangular abstraction meant to tally with a purely imagined light. Poured into the triangular layout so characteristic of his art, instead of dissolving or tending to dissolve form as optical laws lead it to do, this light became a catalytic agent whose role was active and constructive.

Yet, as always with Cézanne, even the most daring procedures were carefully nurtured and guided. Remarking that "with a little spirit and plenty of science one can go far," he never lost sight of the fact that his aim was not to imitate, but to represent, i.e. to build in an entirely new way. Having repudiated conventional formulas, it was up to him to forge out strictly analytical methods by means of which he might test the staying power of the forms and colors in which he dealt. With new objectives in view, new means were imperative.

Nature provided his sensations, i.e. the working materials, but his genius enjoined him not to carry them over to the canvas such as they were, within the measure of skill and acuteness at his command, as did the Impressionists. His sensations—"my little thrill," as he called them—were so intimately a part of him that he meant to control and fashion them as he saw fit.

Possessed by the physical intensity of his feelings, however, he entered a trance-like state as soon as he held the brush in his hands—no doubt the real reason why he hated being watched as he painted. Progressing through a maze of analytical procedures that, try as he might, he could not define, Cézanne contrived to convert his sensations into paints, and once he had begun the picture his source of inspiration was no longer nature herself but the pure sensations she induced in him. What he wanted was to represent nature devoid of a merely visual aspect which, as he saw it, was not really a part of her. Drastically breaking with tradition, he determined to "render perspective by color alone." Even so, for all his magnificent gifts as a colorist, he never surrendered to its charms. Renoir was amazed by Cézanne: "He puts three dabs of color on to his canvas and they fall together perfectly." But Renoir forgot that these initial dabs had been minutely calculated beforehand. In them, for Cézanne himself, the whole picture stood contained, if he could thereafter modulate them—not model them—as his vision dictated. He had practiced modeling of course in his early romantic works, shading off forms progressively in the outmoded academic manner of his day; but now he modulated, i.e. he rendered depth by small dabs and tracts of color of varying intensity.

These were but means to an end, however, since for the time being his efforts were bent to perfecting a technique. We shall see how he finally put this to the service of an aesthetic in which no room was left for empiricism.

YEARS OF EVOLUTION

FROM about 1883 onward, Cézanne's art underwent a change of pace as he brought his keen spirit of analysis to bear less on experimental projects than on practical points of technique that stood within his reach. More and more keenly appreciative of that architectural solidity of whose actual bases he had hitherto had only the vaguest notion, he delved now into the geometrical arcana so fruitfully exploited by the Old Masters.

As we have seen, his passionate addiction to analysis had led him into an intense preoccupation with details and ornamental touches which he had squandered on the picture with true southern prodigality, and certainly exceptional in their convincing, full-bodied, painterly savor. But he gave up nursing the "little thrill" that had infatuated him for a time. Having gained the upper hand in his contest with his sensations, brought them to light and traced their identity, he could henceforth guide and discipline them, strip them of their juvenile animality. Thus his work entered on a new phase of stark purity and simplicity. No longer did it wallow in the rich, pregnant, romantic disorder of previous years. Setting each picture solidly on its feet, he shaped it round a structural framework foursquare, without a rift or flaw. Every part seems to hang together with the next like a flock round the herdsman; the whole is reinforced by such sturdy structural elements as steeples, factory chimneys, trees, roads, viaducts, colonnades of vertical planes in the background of landscapes, backs of chairs and cupboard panels in interiors, the painter's easel in portraits, the upright human body in compositions of nudes—these and many more devices. Another point of interest is Cézanne's systematic elimination of the accidental by linking planes together. To this end he originated procedures which he developed and varied at will, and which the Cubists were to carry even further, namely systems of inter-relationships, re-echoes of stated themes, and correspondences between formal elements that set up rhythms and tempos incomparably rich in poetic overtones.

With relentless persistence Cézanne made his way towards the fullest possible expression of the monumental, a concern that had haunted him in earlier days but which from now on he pushed to an extreme pitch of careful planning, as he called

THE BAY OF MARSEILLES, SEEN FROM L'ESTAQUE, 1883-1885.
(28¾ × 39½″) METROPOLITAN MUSEUM OF ART, NEW YORK.

increasingly on geometry to second his vision, and built on the firm foundations he had detected in nature herself: "the cylinder, cone and sphere." Cautious as always, and making no secret of it, Cézanne the imaginative artist put his faith in geometry —insurance against the excesses of his imagination—as before the man had called upon Rome to steady him on the path of life.

Despite the maturity of his vision and the utter obedience of his hand, Cézanne remained an incurably finical and meticulous artist, fussing over every detail—and there was no changing him. If, as far as themes were concerned, his lifelong preference went to landscapes, the reason was simple: the subject placidly kept its pose, unmoving, unmovable, beneath his vigilant eye. With landscapes he was spared the apprehensions that gnawed at him as he faced the living, breathing model, incapable, of course, of remaining as motionless "as an apple," as he would have liked, while even still lifes obliged him to organize the subject in conjunction with accessories whose choice and arrangement he could never settle to his satisfaction. Then there was his innate fondness for the great out-of-doors, which stimulated his imagination as much as cities and walled-in rooms checked and diluted it. As for his sense of the monumental, never was it more keenly operative than when he found himself inspired by the majestic proportions of a landscape.

We have noted, furthermore, that he showed no interest in the impressionist practice of varying color and light according to the time of day and the course of the sun. His growing attachment to all that was fixed, immobile, static and timeless led him in fact in the opposite direction. His subtly inventive mind increasingly spurned the data of mere observation, however acute and penetrating. What he sought was an invariable, an eternal light in absolute conformity with the logic of the picture. This accounts for his obstinate refusal to mingle tones indiscriminately, his quest of the inevitable color-combinations, of the exact hues and shades, the only ones capable of building planes as he wanted them, exalting light as he conceived it, and conjoining them all in harmonious unity.

It is significant that after 1883 Cézanne turned less and less to the sea as a theme, regarding it as too fluid an element, one incapable of sufficiently galvanizing his passion for colored

GARDANNE, 1885-1886. (31¾ × 25½″)
COLLECTION OF MR AND MRS F. H. HIRSCHLAND, HARRISON, NEW YORK.

GARDANNE AND THE MONTAGNE SAINTE-VICTOIRE, 1885-1886. (24⅝ × 35⅞")
OWNED BY THE UNITED STATES GOVERNMENT.
(FORMERLY IN THE LOESER COLLECTION, FLORENCE)

forms. No more than two or three times, and even then without entire conviction, did he paint the sea stretching limitlessly out to horizon and sky, as the Impressionists were so fond of doing. Except for two views of L'Estaque dating from 1886, Cézanne never painted the sea again, henceforth only rivers—bodies of water, that is, firmly contained within the limits of parallel banks. In this he instinctively followed Baudelaire, whose love

POT OF FLOWERS ON A TABLE, 1882-1887. (23 ½ × 28 ¾")
PELLERIN BEQUEST, LOUVRE, PARIS.

This magnificent still life is like a brilliant anthology of Cézanne's palette, a full description of which was left by the painter Emile Bernard, who, after meeting Cézanne at Aix in 1904, saw much of him, exchanged many letters with the aging master, and was one of the privileged few allowed to stand by and watch him while he painted. Five yellows: glossy yellow, Naples yellow, chrome-yellow, yellow ochre, raw sienna. Six reds: vermilion, red ochre, burnt sienna, madder-red, carmine lake, burnt lake. Three greens: Veronese green, emerald green, terra verde. Three blues: cobalt blue, ultramarine, Prussian blue. And, occasionally, black and white.

BOUQUET AND APPLES, 1883-1887. (21 ½ × 18″)
J. LAROCHE COLLECTION, PARIS.

PORTRAIT OF MADAME CÉZANNE, C. 1885. (18 × 15″)
COLLECTION OF MR AND MRS SAMUEL S. WHITE 3RD, ARDMORE, PA.

went always to canals that contentedly ripple against weir and quay, rather than to the extravagant preenings of the sea. This was the discipline, strictly geometrical, that he now applied to his landscapes: the cone of the Montagne Sainte-Victoire, the cylinders of tree-trunks and roadways, the cubes of farmhouses. All the while, however, he kept clear of any dryness, and having cast powerful doubts on the legitimacy of literally transcribing what the eye sees, he proved that the harmony of the picture need not conform to our habits of seeing, superficial and dulled by custom, but hallowed and inviolable in art until he came on the scene.

In discussing Cézanne's art, most writers agree that, to some extent, every picture he painted may be regarded as a still life. Yet Cézanne can hardly be described as an intimist; he approached a still life exactly as he did a landscape and his technique remained the same in both cases. At first it drew its strength from a battery of horizontals, verticals, parallel lines, angles and triangles, cylinders and spheres. But in his use of color he took care to leave no one in doubt that this was the mainspring of the composition, even in still lifes where he applied it in the slanting, flickering strokes that seemed more suitable to the dynamism of the landscape (he made a point of retaining them for their structural value). He also leaned heavily on a procedure that consisted in stepping up a tone's intensity until brought up short by a contrasting line that defined the form of the object being treated and located it on the picture-surface without immolating it in a display of showy effects—without bodily wrenching it, that is, from the picture-surface, as has since been done by hosts of imitators, with the result that the practice has degenerated into a set formula. These were technical innovations that were to enjoy considerable vogue. And these are only two. Others might be cited here as aptly illustrating the principle that "each side of an object and a plane runs towards a central point." Parallel lines define the horizon and suggest distance, while perpendiculars define spatial depth. Cézanne applied himself to solving the key problem of locating light, form and local tone on a single plane, on an equal footing. Several still lifes of this period show him struggling to hit on exactly the right tone for defining volumes with maximum effect.

Though it lay not far off, he had yet to attain the synthetic plenitude he longed for. The picture-surface remained turbulent, a little overdone with its thick impasto scored with pentimenti. Proceeding by trial and error, Cézanne lingered and fussed over every detail; then, when he finally got what he wanted, he repeatedly tested and varied the result with no concern for the harmony of the picture. Regarding geometry as an instrument of knowledge, he made no attempt to conceal its workings in his pictures, heedless of such discretion.

The striking thing about Cézanne as a portrait-painter is that he attached no importance to bringing out the particular features of his sitters. Yet, having once dictated the pose to be taken, he demanded not only the most absolute immobility —"Does an apple move?" was his implacable reply to their complaints—but frequent and almost interminable sittings. Vollard has vouched for the fact that his portrait required one hundred and forty sittings, and only then did Cézanne grudgingly admit that he was "not dissatisfied with the patch of the shirtfront." The victims of this tyranny were generally the same: his wife, his son, a few complaisant friends, himself if others failed—though he took the pose even less willingly than they to judge from the glumness with which he looks out at us in most of the self-portraits. He troubled little about posing his models in becoming or complicated attitudes, almost always

PORTRAIT OF PAUL CÉZANNE, THE ARTIST'S SON, 1885.
(25 ¾ × 21 ¼″) CHESTER DALE COLLECTION,
NATIONAL GALLERY OF ART, WASHINGTON.

painting them in surrender, idly resigned people looking a little forlorn, not knowing quite what to do with their hands. They might be drowsing; probably they very often were. For Cézanne never sought to capture the reflection in faces of intimate feelings whose play might have enlivened the composition. He claimed for his sitters no more than a kind of bare vegetable existence. The sculptor Despiau summed up a whole school of art when he said: "Out of a portrait I make a head." Cézanne fathered this conception, though his portraits can hardly be called heads either; he showed no more respect for this essential organ than for one of those apples in which his brush seems to have locked all the mysteries of creation.

With his disinterested, painterly approach, Cézanne is usually thought of as quite the reverse of a psychological portraitist. Yet he may well have been capable of treating the model from this angle. Several self-portraits give a fleeting glimpse of the inner man, while the portrait of his friend Victor Chocquet reproduced here is full of the breath of life.

But every figure-painting of this period was a stimulating pretext for technical experiments. With the portrait of Chocquet as a point of departure, we note thereafter a simplified handling of light that frees the composition of the color-masses that had previously weighed it down. Draftsmanship might even be spoken of in this connection. A scrutiny of the faces of his wife and son in their portraits is enough to convince us that, with Cézanne, draftsmanship properly so called is an abstraction, i.e. a means and not an end. Those compositions that seem to be minutely drawn, linework precisely defining form, actually show Cézanne rendering form with the brush. Color and line are one and the same thing for him, since "everything in nature is colored" and "the better the colors match, the more precise

BATHER, 1885-1887. (50×38⅛″) MUSEUM OF MODERN ART, NEW YORK. ▶

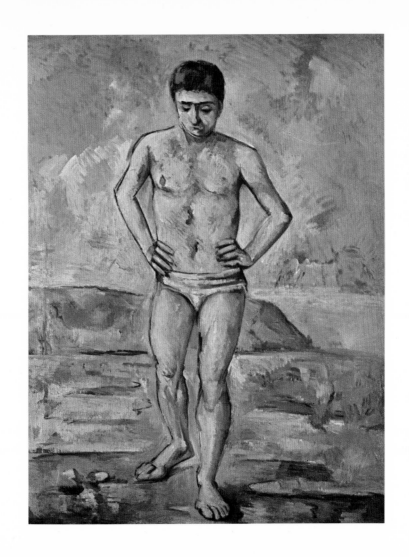

is the linework." But the object of this drawing with the brush remains that of expressing form, and in this Cézanne succeeded so well that all the disembodied elements of geometry he put to use flawlessly blended. The face of his wife is contained in a smooth, immaculate oval whose perfection nothing in the picture disturbs. What is more—and this is too unusual in his work not to be singled out—he keeps to a bare, blue-grey background, hardly modulated at all, which lends a diagrammatical starkness to the composition as a whole. Here, obviously, he stood no more in fear of "too much skill" and plied all the science he could summon up against the old naïveté. In the portraits of this period we find none of those childish lapses into awkwardness, none of the outright blundering that marred so many of his youthful works. At the Louvre, in the course of his visits to Paris, the masters not only revealed their trade-secrets to him, but opened his eyes to the meaning of "style." After the Venetians, the Spaniards and even the Bolognese, who appealed to his sensuality and his love of fine texture, he discovered his countryman Nicolas Poussin, whose work, as he soon came to realize, was that of a man whose gifts and aims were much like his own.

Whenever Cézanne painted such isolated nude figures as this *Bather*, he did so in a vein of straightforward realism unusual in his work, whose importance, however, is hardly more than incidental. This occasional contact with the human anatomy kept him from straying too far towards abstraction. Thus we have such drawings and sketches as those executed round about 1860 in his early academic period, or those, much more freely handled, dating from about 1875. The isolated nudes he now painted strike the same attitudes later to be found in the large compositions of bathers, for which in fact they were taken over bodily when at last he felt ready for those soaring rhythms of transcendental forms. But in the big male nude reproduced here, realism is no longer carried to an extreme as it was in many an earlier drawing of the same theme. Its static pose issues straight from Cézanne's preoccupation with constructive geometry, which accounts for the perpendicular squarely planted on the horizontal and the abundance of angles, triangles, spheres and cylinders. Glimpsing true style ahead, he strove towards it with all his might. So doing, he made his way back to the purest classical tradition, probably without consciously realizing it.

The fact is that the problem of the nude, with Cézanne, was a problem of composition; the mere expression of his animal spirits was a thing of the past. Just as he put tones together with a view to rendering the volumes he wanted, and to no other end, so from now on the human body became a convenient assemblage of planes and masses lending themselves to the pictorial architecture he had in mind. (Mallarmé defined this kind of art when he protested that poetry was made with words, not with ideas.) As we see in the *Bathers* reproduced here, when Cézanne merges his nudes with the other elements of the picture, the result is a monumental impression of unity. Having resolutely done away with the accidental all along the line, he achieves an architectural simplicity unrivaled in its grandeur. He made a minor concession to his smoldering sensuality, but certainly a forgivable one, in bestowing graceful attitudes on his nudes, but these, too, were to go by the board in a few years' time. Not that Cézanne was making an effort to please; this was simply a lingering trace of the representational art with which he was surrounded. The grace of a movement remains in keeping with the delicacy of the tones. But there was more to it than that with Cézanne, and the Dionysian inspiration behind his *Bathers* remains rigorously ordered. And though their stalwart figures have all the sweep of a dynamic ballet, every movement and attitude, however free in appearance, is strictly disciplined.

HARLEQUIN, 1888-1890. (36⅛ × 25½")
COLLECTION OF LORD VICTOR ROTHSCHILD, CAMBRIDGE, ENGLAND.

THE SYNTHESIS

B Y 1888-1890 Cézanne stood in full possession of his means, and his painting breathed a mature, serene simplicity in stark contrast with the storm and strain so obvious in much of his earlier work. The reason for this was twofold, lying both in the solid technical proficiency he had acquired and in the more settled way of life he had entered on.

He had always worked slowly and made his way ahead step by careful step, never in fine bursts of inspiration, while the vicissitudes of his private life had invariably been complicated by his irascible temper. The fact is that Cézanne had turned fifty before enjoying peace and quiet, and before making his name as an artist. He had long since grown accustomed to the sneers and condescension of those who took him for a crank sadly afflicted with astigmatism, and even his own doubts had become a kind of second nature with which he stood on familiar (if never very affable) terms.

In 1886, upon his father's death, he came into a considerable fortune. Thereafter he practically ceased to travel. He settled in Paris for a year in 1888, then returned to Aix where he spent the next five years, in peaceful isolation, painting daily. He made some new and notable friends, among them Van Gogh and Gauguin (the works of both men irritated him, however), and met Clemenceau and Rodin. His inferiority complex as well as his superiority complex—he suffered from both—led him humbly to thank the latter—"a man who has been decorated"— for having shaken his hand. The most enlightened critics of the day began to realize the significance of his art and wrote in praise of it. Invited to exhibit with "Les Vingt" at Brussels in 1887, he felt flattered and hastened to accept. Then he showed at the Décennale (1889) and at the Indépendants (1899). Though frowned on by the dignitaries of the Institut de France,

MOUNTAINS IN PROVENCE, 1886-1890. (25½ × 31¾″)
BY COURTESY OF THE TRUSTEES, NATIONAL GALLERY, LONDON.

This composition inaugurates a new phase of expression in Cézanne's art, as we see him radically condensing and simplifying his means in keeping with an atmosphere of serenity that made all problems seem remote and irrelevant. The rugged barrage of volumes in the foreground is apparently made up of well-staggered units, but these are indissolubly linked together by the swelling, communicative richness of their texture. Planes stand broadly, securely in place, no sign of doubt or hesitation left. Having come into his own as far as technical mastery is concerned, Cézanne felt so sure of himself that an incidental note of bravura has crept into this work.

Nothing could be finer or purer than the luminous, crystalline simplicity of this composition, in which every element, reduced to the essence of its form, rings true and delights the eye. Here, as in the preceding landscape, he wipes the sky clean of accidental streakings and puffs of cloud, and a bracing air of classicism blows through the entire canvas. The foreground is a broad, uniform band of warm orange ochre, while the sky billows out in the cool, intense blue no traditional landscape can do without. This, however, never prevented Cézanne, when the inclination took him, from reversing the roles of these two colors, as the Impressionists often did.

PIGEON TOWER AT MONTBRIAND, 1888-1892. (25 ¼ × 31 ½")
MUSEUM OF ART, CLEVELAND.

the Caillebotte Bequest, including several Cézannes, was at last accepted by the Musée du Luxembourg, and Cézanne to his amazement—and intense satisfaction—found his canvases hanging in the same august galleries as those by Bouguereau and company. In 1895 Vollard organized a large-scale Cézanne exhibition at his picture-shop in the Rue Laffitte: one hundred

MILK-JUG AND FRUIT ON A TABLE, 1888-1890. (23 ½ × 28⅝″)
NATIONAL GALLERY, OSLO.

STILL LIFE WITH APPLES AND PRIMROSES, 1890-1894. (28⅜ × 36½″)
METROPOLITAN MUSEUM OF ART, NEW YORK.

This still life belonged for many years to Monet, who bought it in 1894
almost as soon as Cézanne had finished it. In the poetic motionlessness of
this quiet gathering of flowers, leaves and apples, Cézanne found an ideal
opportunity to indulge in subtle shadings of tones: reds and yellows turn
imperceptibly into orange and green, giving rise to delicate harmonies.
He worked slowly here, cleaning his brush after each stroke so as to get
a thin, uniform layer of paint, over which he painted again once it was
dry—a method that greatly contributed to the durability of the canvas.

and fifty canvases. Gérôme, Ferrier and Puvis de Chavannes solemnly protested, invoking the dignity of art and the respect owed it, while jeering crowds gathered at the gallery windows and near-riots broke out. At the Centennial Exhibition of the Paris World's Fair in 1900 Roger Marx succeeded in entering three pictures by Cézanne, while Bouguereau and Cabanel were allowed but one each. Hitherto only a few fellow artists had bought his works, notably Degas and Monet, but now they were sought after by such connoisseurs as Auguste Pellerin, Count Camondo and King Milan of Serbia. The surest sign of his success, however, was the fact that his neighbors at Aix no longer dismissed him as a harmless eccentric, but looked up to him now as a shrewd old fellow who had put one over on the Parisians.

His reputation established, his self-confidence was restored and this was reflected in his art. His long-standing obsession with a strictly analytical approach gave way to a coordination of means that made for a simpler, more serene form of expression, embodying the classicism he had always longed to achieve.

If we examine in detail the landscapes first of all, we notice that Cézanne tended more and more to sweep his skies clear of the fleecy clouds he had hitherto bunched together in vaguely romantic masses that served as a very conventional expression of light. And instead of intensifying the mosaic of tiny cubes of contrasting color, which he had heavily depended on and even exploited, Cézanne thinned them out and toned them down. He no longer painted with so full a brush, nor kneaded his impasto into fine, elusive configurations of jewel-like tones. With a light laying on of pigment he got the same results and more, notably those subtly reflected gleams within gleams, which, alike in values, he sowed over the entire picture-surface. In other words, Cézanne plainly felt no need now to commit

MADAME CÉZANNE IN THE CONSERVATORY, C. 1890. (36 ¼ × 28 ¾″)
STEPHEN C. CLARK COLLECTION, NEW YORK.

his energies to the experiments that had long absorbed him; these having borne fruit, he stood assured of the solid technical means that went hand in hand with his imagination, wedding its visions with passionate alacrity.

Cézanne once admitted to Zola that he had "come late to nature," who had not waited in vain, however, for he endowed her with a majestic grandeur whose secrets he had been jealously guarding, pending the day when he might "spring" them to best effect. That day came with his synthetic period, when, ever more classically minded, ever more sparing of his means, he attained the unity that characterized his work from this time on and smoothed out the unevenness, the brittle inequalities of which his previous work had not always been free. His so-called distortions—wobbly tables, drunken bottles, trauma-stricken vases—may not always seem logically constructed, and perhaps out of defiance, whimsy, rage or derring-do he some-times exaggerated the scope of a line or the depth of a tone, especially in his "witchhunt" for those famous, virtually inexistent contour-lines he could never quite seize on to his satisfaction. But he had come to terms with reality, having at last understood that the painter's way of seeing may very well stand at variance with that of ordinary people, that pictorial architecture may very well comply with other laws of form than those of the master-builder, and this as a result of those mira-culous plays of color by which volumes are kept in balance.

This knowledge, coupled with technical mastery of the finest order, gave a revolutionary flavor to what had once seemed mere awkwardness, which he himself had angrily recognized as such in his letters to Zola, cursing the heavens for it with unblushing blasphemy. Awkwardness it may in part have been at first, but beneath the serried squares and cubes of color, beneath the feverish, "astigmatic" brushwork, the true vein of his genius coursed. What he succeeded in imparting to it now was a saving grace and mellowness completely unexpected in the "boor" Cézanne in many ways never ceased to be. A gracefulness whose constituent elements were an almost apologetic gaucherie, discreetly disguised errors and stumblings cleverly redressed. For even Cézanne's mature style was the offspring, however remote, of an ineradicable awkwardness, never affected, but perfectly natural, on the contrary.

CARD PLAYER, 1890-1892. (14¼×19″)
WATERCOLOR. CHAUNCEY MCCORMICK COLLECTION, CHICAGO.

CARD PLAYERS, 1890-1892. (25⅝ × 31⅞″)
STEPHEN C. CLARK COLLECTION, NEW YORK.

This picture, one of five painted on the same theme, draws in its turn on the deep vein of realism that runs through all French art. With their rustic simplicity, the eloquent warmth and sobriety of the tones, their static posture, these peasants, each stolidly absorbed in his hand of cards, re-echo the immemorial Gallic and Romanesque tradition of French realism.

◄　　WOMAN WITH A COFFEE-POT, 1890-1894. (51 × 38″)
PRIVATE COLLECTION, PARIS.

The great still lifes of this period show him purifying and simplifying forms, and doing so eloquently. In them, as in many portraits, he forewent every non-essential to the point of skeletal starkness, saved from bleakness only by his color. Objects became few and far between, light and air moving amongst them with sovereign ease and amplitude. But there was nothing arbitrary about these measures—"I see more lucidly into nature," was how he explained it. What were his step-by-step syntheses but the patient search for an underlying unity and simplicity? And as he neared them, he erred less and less in his own eyes and could push on steadily without scraping, painting out, beginning the picture anew or angrily throwing it into the fire, as he had so often done in the past. He ceased leaving parts of the canvas blank in his conscientious perplexity as how best to bring them into line with what he had already painted. Not that he worked ahead rapidly, always Cézanne painted with extreme deliberation; but he fell to casting about far less now that his visions drew unfailingly on their raw material: his sensations. He visualized the picture in his mind, and visualized it synthetically in relation to the means he knew he could bring to bear. His grasp on the structural design of the picture firm and confident, he had only to build thereon in keeping with the essential character of that design, which he himself had conceived.

The still lifes best reveal the visual aspect of this geometrical design or framework. The composition of the picture had gained immensely in suppleness and freedom, mellowed by a subtle, all-pervading elegance. Straight lines had lost their rigor, curving inward softly, stealthily, much as Greek architects softened the base lines of pediments by curving them almost imperceptibly. Thus Cézanne no longer sought the stylization he had coveted and practiced in his constructive period, no longer subordinated the elements of the picture to geometrical

STILL LIFE WITH A PLASTER CAST, C. 1895. (24¾ × 31¾″)
NATIONAL MUSEUM, STOCKHOLM.

Here the artist has assembled all the elements he required for a severely pyramidal composition, based this time on the central figure of a small statue instead of a bather. But he seems to have yielded to a temptation to express what he *feels* rather than sacrificing this to what he *sees*, which is almost invariably what he sets out to do. For the moment, however, as if taking up a challenge, he covers the canvas with a variety of blues broken down into overlapping tones that, in their way, recall the superposing of forms he is led to practice in his attempts "to wed the curves of women's bodies to the shoulders of hills."

BOY IN A RED WAISTCOAT, 1890-1895. (36¼ × 28¾″)
PRIVATE COLLECTION, ZURICH.

shapes. Instead of going towards geometry, for having so diligently assimilated its workings and practical effects he now started out from it implicitly. And, as luck would have it, geometry came to him naturally enough for the life of the picture to be enhanced and empowered by it without ever betraying the mechanics of the operation.

A similar evolution took place in the case of his figure-paintings, for here his rankling obsession with contour-lines set him problems his instinct was incapable of solving alone. Why this obsession? It is no easy matter getting down to the real reasons for it, but his entire career is punctuated by his impatient outcries against the "contours that melt away." In some corner of his heart, no doubt, he secretly envied the smooth precision and finish of Bouguereau's pictures. In one sense Cézanne never quite worked the rough edges off his own landscapes, and die-hard provincial that he was, with a classical schooling grafted on to him, he always had a secret hankering after respectability, a secret envy of established academic doctrines and their highly touted perfections. Fortunately, without his even being aware of it, his genius steered him unscathed through this life-long ambush of yearnings and temptations. It saved him, furthermore, from falling under the spell of Ingres' knife-sharp outlines, a hardy extreme for which he much admired that master, but a solution his instinct would have none of ("Your Dominique is as clever as they come, but he's no help at all," he wrote in a letter). Cézanne was not long in realizing that, for him at least, linear contours only served to pinch and strangle form, to repress the voluptuous expansion he felt form longed for, and which he liberally gave it in the exercise of his invincible penchant for "distortion." Something told him that by sticking to the literal side of things he would never get on intimate terms either with reality or art; thus he chose the subtler way. Cézanne's eye—if the expression be permitted—blindly obeyed the artist in him, whose insight went deeper and whose inspirations soared beyond earthbound conventions and conformism. The man and the painter were continually contending, but the latter never lost an encounter or ceased to gain headway. As the painter exploited these successes, we see the outlines of objects breaking, crumbling, overflowing, flouting the common sense of the academicians. He took liberties right and left, proceeding by bold leaps and bounds, by excess and compensation, inching out with a line on the one hand, lashing out with a full brush on the other. All this, in his own day, was chalked up to clumsiness by most, while others, keeping faith with the punctilio and niceties of academic forms, deplored Cézanne's surrender to "baroque"—a mild term that falls far too short of describing his wonderful faculty of sweeping aside appearances and bringing to light such hidden relationships as confirm and enhance the thrilling authenticity of beautiful things.

The surest sign that Cézanne in his synthetic period at last acceded to his mature style is the fact that he had got over his fascination for the outward particularities of objects. While hitherto he tended to approach the object under the spell of purely visual enchantments, he came now so completely to focus his mind on it that he had no need of eyes to draw aside the veil of its innermost life and freely elicit from it the hidden light that before he had had to confer on it with whatever artifice he stood in possession of. Thus he came to paint imagined figures, still lifes and landscapes located on a flat plane of space much like that screen on which objects loom up in the memory, which simplifies, schematizes, synthesizes. Cézanne was no longer out to paint what seemed objectively true, but to capture something purely visionary and subjective. So it is that while

The bathers of this composition still continue the vein of traditional realism we observed in the *Card Players*. And where academic critics once saw only awkwardness and fumbling, we see today the true-to-life attitudes, never idealized, of these nudes as they relax and exercise in the open air. The lay-out of this work still abides by the truncated pyramid, which he had already put to such good use. The arms and legs of the seated bather on the far left, moreover, provide a typical example of rhythmic parallels, while the diagonal of his forward-leaning body together with that of the lunging bather on the right form the two arrises of the pyramid.

BATHERS, 1892-1894. $(23\frac{1}{2} \times 31\frac{3}{4}'')$
COLLECTION OF BARON NAPOLÉON GOURGAUD, PARIS.

BATHERS, C. 1895. (10⅝ × 18⅛″)
CONE COLLECTION, MUSEUM OF ART, BALTIMORE.

With this work Cézanne entered on a final phase of exaltation that saw him disembody objects to the point of coining abstract forms and figures which, with the tip of his brush, he swept up in colors that glowed with the deep, infectious pleasure he took in handling them.

a certain expression of life still clung to the earlier portraits, those of the present period were but faint allusions to models who doubtless sat for him days and weeks on end, but in vain, we might say; he saw them only with the mind's eye, and they were no more to him than random or isolated components of a world whose fellow components were the other patient, familiar objects, few in number now, with which he peopled his canvases over and over again.

Yet the fact remains: for all their strict and flawless architecture, for all their geometrical stylization, Cézanne's figures and genre scenes such as the *Card Players*, a favorite theme to which he reverted a number of times, reflect a deep and genuine feeling for the soil, and for those who work it and depend on its fruit. This communion with nature and peasant life underlies Cézanne's art as it has underlaid all French art from time immemorial. Indifferent to the sophistications of city-dwellers, he responded at once to the earthiness and rude simplicity of the French peasantry, whose soul was his own. Hence, for one thing, the attitudes of people in his figure-paintings, invariably devoid of any prettiness, refinement, or mannerism. They stand there stiffly, like the hieratic idols of Byzantine art whose arabesques, however, he replaced by a balance of volumes no less abstract. Or they sit in inflexible postures, as do the *Card Players*, whose two-dimensional architecture links up with that of the Romanesque fresco-painters. But if Cézanne's peasants still pulse with all the life that was reduced to mere symbol by the Byzantine artist, and if they retain the vigor and vitality of Romanesque and Gothic figures, the reason is that Cézanne fell quite naturally into line with a tradition that forms the indispensable background of all painting truly French in spirit. However strong the periodic influence of Italy, French art has never faltered in its attachment to nature, to the soil, to the realities—both peasant and bourgeois—that have made that art what it is today: the rich heir of a hearty, healthy realism whose vigorous exponents have followed one another uninterruptedly from the great cathedral sculptors and the Romanesque *imagiers* to Fouquet, Pol de Limbourg, the brothers Le Nain, Chardin, Courbet, Millet, Daumier, the Impressionists and many more recent artists—a galaxy in which Cézanne's place is as secure as any. In fact he may well have been the most deeply sincere of them all.

The scenes of bathers prove his admiration for Poussin, whose art was as stupidly cried down in its day as Cézanne's was in his. For this master, whom Delacroix regarded as a revolutionary, Cézanne towards the end of his life conceived a passion that left room for no one else in his esteem. And this fact will help us to understand the classical nature of Cézanne's way of seeing. Instead of welding the picture elements into established anecdotal patterns, he combined and superposed them in the manner of Poussin so as to elicit formal rhythms, a prosody of forms that had little or nothing to do with descriptive realism. With such figure-paintings as the *Card Players* he put an end to a type of expression he had long cultivated, whose undertones of poetry were as strictly held in check as those of prose in the classical alexandrines of Racine. No such disciplined solemnity in the pictures of bathers. These are the murmured confidings of the brush, discreet and intimate modulations of color, never so limpid before, flowing arabesques deeply, incalculably serene. As for the bathers themselves, no more importance is attached to their actual figures than to those of Polyphemus, Hercules and Diogenes, which melt away into the landscape paradise painted by Poussin.

In an often quoted phrase Cézanne gave it out as his ambition to "do Poussin over again after nature." And though there is no denying Poussin's love of nature—too great and exclusive a love, in fact, in the eyes of his contemporaries—obviously neither he nor Cézanne saw her in quite the same spirit. But this much may be said: Cézanne followed in Poussin's footsteps when he set out to re-create the cosmos in a form that both rejected the heady visions of a facile, impeachable idealism and transcended the data of ocular observation—a form that bared and brought into play the generative elements of life itself. And in the works of his last years this vivid sense of life never ceased to gain in intensity and exultation.

THE LAST YEARS

THE last ten years of his life saw Cézanne, now aging fast, enveloped in a mesh of sentiments and circumstances that deeply affected both his manner of living and the ultimate trend of his art.

His sturdy constitution had been broken by the inroads of diabetes, and by the time he was sixty (in 1899) he looked at least ten years older. Then, too, there was the death of his mother (1897), a cruel blow to him, for she was the one person in the world he loved with an entire heart, and who returned his love. He sold the Jas de Bouffan and, entering on a lonely, hermit-like existence, took a small flat in town at Aix, looked after there by an elderly housekeeper who had all she could do to bear with his endless complaints and browbeatings. No less restless than peevish, he changed houses a number of times, then finally rented a cottage in the Bibemus Quarry, outside Aix. The sonorous name of the place—whose Latin ring evokes not only his student years but also the drinking-bouts boisterous youths are given to—has come to designate a phase of fresh inspiration and surprises in his evolution. In 1904 he had a studio built on the outskirts of Aix, in the Chemin des Lauves, and here he worked on uninterruptedly until his death.

The only peace and satisfaction the old man found, needless to say, were in his art and the triumphs it was now scoring. A very relative satisfaction, however, that in the end did little more than embitter him. He saw the Berlin Museum go out of its way to purchase one of his landscapes. Then, after the death of Victor Chocquet, when his old friend's collection went up for sale, his pictures fetched unexpectedly high prices: four thousand four hundred francs for his *Mardi Gras*, six thousand seven hundred for *Melting Snow at L'Estaque*. Maurice Denis painted his *Homage to Cézanne*, a tribute that touched him deeply. Poets

At this period Cézanne's art was beginning to move beyond the strict disciplines of analysis and synthesis. Having assimilated the constructive virtues of geometry, he could do away with its outward shell. He lashes the elements of this landscape into a dynamism of forms and colors that owes practically nothing to the observation of nature. Did we not know him better, we might conclude that his brush had run away with his hand in a mad play of light-paths, whose patterns show every sign of being improvised. Anyhow the picture retains all the fine spontaneity of a sketch.

TALL PINE, 1892-1896. (33⅜ × 36¼")
MUSEU DE ARTE, SAO PAULO, BRAZIL.

LE CHATEAU NOIR, 1894-1896. (28⅝ × 36⅛″)
OSKAR REINHART COLLECTION, WINTERTHUR.

and painters of the younger generation made the pilgrimage
to Aix to see him and express their admiration—Emile Bernard,
Charles Camoin, Maurice Denis, K. X. Roussel. Leo Larguier,
Marc Lafargue, Edmond Jaloux. With several of these men he
exchanged letters that afford precious insight into his views
and methods of work. Another agreeable surprise came with

LA MONTAGNE SAINTE-VICTOIRE, SEEN FROM BIBEMUS, 1898.
(25 ½ × 32″) CONE COLLECTION, MUSEUM OF ART, BALTIMORE.

This work gives a good idea of the distance covered by the artist since his *Gardanne and the Montagne Sainte-Victoire* of 1885-1886, reproduced on page 69. Still the more or less descriptive image of a panorama, the latter ran on traditional lines of which no trace now remains. All is allusion here, bold and discreet at once, expressed in a pictorial syntax of Cézanne's own creation. We have a notable instance of his "flat depth" in the hollow space between the righthand slope of the mountain and the jagged color-patch opposite it, which may or may not be cloud. Obviously Cézanne felt the magnetic if intermittent appeal of a chaotic view of nature.

the 1904 Salon d'Automne: an entire room was set aside for his work, with thirty-three canvases shown. The exhibition met with complete success and he was hailed as the Modern Master whose coming had been so long awaited. But this recognition, after half a century's work, must have seemed sadly belated in his own eyes, though in a letter to his young friend Joachim Gasquet he wrote, with instinctive foresight: "Perhaps I have come too soon... I was the painter of your generation more than my own... I am growing old... and shall not have the time to express myself fully."

The upshot of these events that crowded in upon him—his illness, his premature old age, the acclamation of his genius by the artistic élite of his day—was, if anything, to speed up his activities, to make him paint harder, more intensely than ever before, and this despite the fact that he had always been an unrelenting worker. He held out valiantly against illness, and far from being content merely to stand on his laurels, experienced a fresh spurt of creative energy whose tempestuous exaltation harked back to the excitements of his romantic period.

Some artists grow old gracefully, while others do not. Those who age well, instead of spinning out the old inspirations interminably, or cultivating some harmless form of senility, somehow seem to complete the circle; they take a second breath, renewing, it would seem, the turbulent ambitions of their youth, but voicing them now with an effortless power that no youthful painter can hope to achieve. So it was with the late Cézanne. His last works are a kind of Indian summer, an ineffable swan-song, from which a note of almost desperate abandon escapes, as if he had been driven to stake everything on this final expression of his powers, well aware that he had nothing to lose. Did he scent the approach of an ideal perfection he had never dared dream of hitherto, or was this a regal indifference to all that others had taught him, as now he let the eagle soar, giving a

ONIONS AND BOTTLE, 1895-1900. (26 × 20″) LOUVRE, PARIS.

An unusual work for Cézanne, in which he seems to amuse himself by piling up a helter-skelter agglomeration of objects from which all the loose ends protrude—in the form of onions's tails, with a knife-handle and the neck of a bottle thrown in on either side. At various points we detect our liberator of forms at work: the cunningly distorted sides of the bottle, the odd tilt given the plate at the corner of the table, the stem of the glass deliberately thrown off-center, all of which herald the ruthless synthesis objects were soon to undergo at the hands of the Cubists—still tempered here by the delicate lines of the table and the plain background.

Whenever he thought a risk had been run long enough, Cézanne retraced his steps and secured his positions. Having broken up forms and strode into the near-abstract, as we have seen in the preceding pages, he felt it time to call a halt to these audacities and sought an antidote in such fine, solidly constructed still lifes as this. The ripe wisdom of his old age, true wisdom that it was, could still revive the enthusiasms of his youth. Hence this glowing array of smoothly blended tones parading the resources of his palette and filling the canvas with opulent forms and colors.

STILL LIFE WITH APPLES, 1895-1900. (27 × 36½″)
LILY P. BLISS COLLECTION, MUSEUM OF MODERN ART, NEW YORK.

free hand to the unbridled ego that broke his last ties with nature. Like every master at the twilight of his career, he found himself on a lonely path, but one that, up to the very end, he still trod with his customary pauses for breath, though plainly he disengaged his art from every incidental, every accessory, chiseling it down to the supreme crystalline purity that marked the goal of a lifetime's efforts: pure painting. By this is meant that, like those of his old friends Monet and Renoir, Cézanne's last works break over the border into a realm of abstract forms and colors, where hand and brush move in mindless unison.

From 1895 on, his landscapes took a distinct turn towards greater dynamism and intensity. After the pregnant serenity of *Mountains in Provence* and *Pigeon Tower at Montbriand*, both reproduced here, came preludes of a frenzy of formal patterns that rose in pitch from day to day, sweeping off the canvas the static color-constructions of his synthetic period. The straight lines whose sturdy building properties he had so much depended on gave way to free-flowing curves that now rose and fell in harmony, now unleashed a wave of counter-rhythms. In the *Montagne Sainte-Victoire* (1885) we have lines and planes that partition a picture-surface crammed with mosaic-like touches and tiny cubic masses tightly "inlaid" with minute care. Turning to the *Montagne Sainte-Victoire* of 1898 we find a completely different type of composition: a schematic arrangement of planes that broaden out in a flat perspective that expresses volumes less by varying touches than by patches of color quite arbitrary by the standards of the eye, but full of fresh and unexpected poetry. The tones themselves run together in a succession of translucent shadings bounded by outlines whose contrasts are set in keys increasingly subdued. Obviously Cézanne was out to free himself of the bondage imposed by geometry, a bondage he had struggled against only very mildly in the immediate past.

MAN WITH A PIPE LEANING ON A TABLE, 1895-1900. $(36\frac{1}{4} \times 28\frac{3}{4}'')$
KUNSTHALLE, MANNHEIM.

Even the still lifes of this period reveal his break with the simplifications resorted to in the years 1888-1890. A comparison of the two still lifes from the Louvre and the Museum of Modern Art with those of the synthetic period is rewarding. The latter, as we see at a glance, are simpler, starker, more concentrated; in a sense they are like demonstrations of a geometrical theorem. The former are fuller, more opulent, swelling with richly colored charms. Cézanne knew what he was about; this was a deliberate movement towards increasing volume, stacking up forms that tumble over one another and defy the graceful proportions of geometry. In *Onions and Bottle* the flattened spheres of fresh vegetables, unusual in Cézanne's still lifes, hang retiringly from long stems that are like whimsical tails stressing the casual freedom of the composition, while the classical roundness of his apples comes in for distortion too. Then there is the top of the glass, distinctly "cubist," as is the steeply inclined table-top, bold steps both, and lessons in artistry that were not to be lost on the coming generation.

With *Onions and Bottle* only finished in 1900, we stand on the threshold of the new century in which Cézanne's message took effect on the new school of painters, whose revolutionary achievements, after his own death, his friends Monet and Renoir lived on to see and marvel at.

SEATED PEASANT, 1900-1904. $(17\frac{3}{4} \times 11\frac{3}{4}'')$ ►
WATERCOLOR. KUNSTHAUS, ZURICH.

Cézanne attached so little importance to the psychological interpretation of his models that one day, the old peasant having failed to turn up for the sitting, he donned the clothes himself and took up the pose in his stead. The inspiration of an eccentric perhaps, but here is the result: a delicately brushed watercolor whose keen spontaneity issues from an ensemble of rugged volumes poised in serene harmony, every extraneous element banished. The inventive power of the work is surpassed only by its utter simplicity of expression.

III

PORTRAIT OF VALLIER, 1906. (25 ½ × 21 ¼″)
PAUL ROSENBERG COLLECTION, PARIS

Cézanne's Italian background may account for the state of poetic grace in which, in varying degrees, he lived all his life, and which, saving his eye from the commonplaces of visual observation, pointed the way to that visionary freedom so wonderfully seconded by the promptings of his "little thrill." However insignificant a stimulus it seemed, it culminated in such gorgeous color-constructions as the chaos of volumes he elicited from the cataclysmic rock-formations of the Bibemus Quarry, from the clearings of Fontainebleau Forest, from the phantasmal silhouette of the Château Noir or the flat, mysterious depths of the trees and forest interiors he painted over and over again. For all we can tell, he had forgotten the technical experiments of old. With nothing left either to teach or to learn, for having savored every feeling and sensation he could now embrace the fullness of his art. His means at his fingertips, he worked on with no other eye than that of the mind, a pure eye, a perfect instrument that dispensed him from every concern for technique and style. In earlier days he had said: "The sensations of color induced by light lead to abstractions that prevent me from filling up the canvas and fixing objects when the points of contact are so tenuous and delicate; my vision of the picture is therefore incomplete." The late Cézanne had ceased to fear the abstract. What did it matter now if objects failed to be "fixed" on the canvas? Let them fend for themselves amid a sparkling array of tones, intense beyond anything seen in his work before.

◀   PORTRAIT OF VALLIER.

Cézanne always stood out against the influence of the sitter and in fact overrode it easily once the picture was underway. This portrait of his gardener Vallier is a model of what might almost be termed elaborate simplicity. The work seems to have begun from a fairly realistic point of departure, but as always with him, what began as observation ended up as the creation of new form. We cannot help feeling, moreover, that the sitter's jumper, especially the left sleeve, interested him more than the old man himself.

In such final works as the *Château Noir* and the *Cabanon de Jourdan* (unfinished at his death) the "primitive of a new art," as he called himself, paid scant heed to contours and transitions, dealing exclusively in a brilliant patchwork of color-rhythms carried to a disembodied extreme of pictorial abstraction.

Also unfinished at his death, the *Grandes Baigneuses* occupied him off and on for the last seven years of his life and may be regarded as his artistic testament and an anthology of forms and poetry in his work. It brings out his conception of pictorial architecture in all its monumental boldness, all its full-bodied poetry. Cézanne lived out his old age in the shadow of this painting, which he kept beside him in his studio, no doubt as a kind of reference work.

The whole canvas is bathed in that atmospheric blue which, for Cézanne, radiated light and space. But the imbricate surface of old, the overlapping planes of color, have given way to the limpid, delicate brushwork of his watercolors. It is the same translucency he had taken up in his *Woman with a Fur* of 1879, when he was seeking an antidote to impressionist sophistries. Master of himself now, he reduced his palette to two basic colors, blue and orange ochre, broken down into half-tints alternately warm and cool, shaded off so as to suggest light. Here we have all the noble thrift and simplicity of the born colorist who, abstaining from every show of superficial brilliance, revealed his secret when he said: "The chief thing is a neutral point of departure."

The actual building of the picture consists of setting up rhythms of pyramids repeated on all sides with the insistence of a leitmotiv. Now more than ever Cézanne held geometry as expressive of the essence of form. This conviction is coupled here with the poetic instinct that had so often led him to build in terms of pyramids, which to him were a symbol of man's and matter's aspiration towards the infinity of the heavens.

Cézanne worked over this large-scale composition for some seven years, and even so cannot be said to have finished it. The picture is rightly regarded, however, as his finest exposition of the classicism to which he gave new life, new form, new poetry. He had been painting bathers since 1875, but here he sums up all of them—the last and greatest fruit of his self-proclaimed method of work: "to carry on without believing in any-one." Never were his architectonic rhythms purer and grander, never more glowing the blues that, after so many restless years, promise peace at last.

LES GRANDES BAIGNEUSES, 1898-1905. (82 × 98″)
WILSTACH COLLECTION, MUSEUM OF ART, PHILADELPHIA.

Cézanne furthermore proved—if proof were needed—that there was nothing random about his contour-lines, nothing of either true or false inspiration in their genesis; they were the outcome, on the contrary, of careful planning and ripe reflection. Which may also prove that his drawings were finished works of art in their own right rather than the mere working sketches they are usually assumed to be.

With the *Grandes Baigneuses*, an "historical" landscape of a kind Poussin never dreamt of, Cézanne induces in the spectator an emotion based on form alone, and partaking in its way of the faith renewed or inspired by the religious works of the Primitives. But here the pyramidal lay-out is everything, the whole picture being conceived in terms of a rhythm of parallels that tend to run together but are cut off by the picture-frame before they get far. The same truncated pyramid occurs in various disguises in every picture of the *Montagne Sainte-Victoire*. What Cézanne asked of geometry, as we have noted, was the subtle collaboration of its vital, constructive essence, not the mere patterns of its forms. Yet, for reasons obscure, his temperament seems to have led him constantly to toy with the idea that, since parallels by definition can never meet, the game of suggesting their eventual union, and nearly provoking it, is all the more fascinating. He played on this suggestive note with subtle variations, hinting at the dramas hanging fire at the unseen point in outer space where the meeting occurs. These parallels flow through his pictures like the irreconcilable banks of a river that finally sink away into the sea, unknown each to each. Something of this fatality stirs in the *Grandes Baigneuses*, with its trees as tensely flexed as the flying buttresses of a Gothic cathedral. Light and color, like the breezes of nature, may make their leafage mingle, but the trunks can never merge. Their suggested merging, however, greatly contributes to the tension and density which here, as in all great art, are superbly achieved.

These frustrated parallels reflect Cézanne's life, the solitary, restless life of a man who—fortunately for art, perhaps—never found the satisfactions he coveted. Brush in hand every day, prospecting a region where he never quite struck the ideal vein whose possible existence haunted him, he nevertheless produced a body of work whose revolutionary beauties he created virtually out of nothing, and whose impact on those who came after him is far from having worked itself out.

This is the eternal quest of genius, and throws light on the inner workings of that phenomenon. Any number of artists, among them some of the greatest, have owned to being never quite sure of themselves, and expressed their surprise at the intentions critics read into everything they do. Though he often spoke and wrote of his methods and aims, Cézanne could never describe them adequately, while we may feel certain that, for all the methodical diligence behind it, his genius reaped the benefit of many an unlooked-for discovery. The stuff of intuition lies perhaps in the vague associations that flash into mind when least expected and transmute established values into revolutionary measures. Genius is not genius when it fails to transgress the order of things to invent another order such as the principle of nature-imitation could never give rise to. Not to speak of the strange sights that have welled up on painters' canvases, the field of mechanics, for example, is full of curious discoveries—the wheel, whose coming at the dawn of prehistory settled then and there the direction man's progress was to take, or, in our own time, the invention of the propellor.

The point to be made here, as far as Cézanne is concerned, is this: whatever his debt to traditional aesthetic, the fact remains that out of his own sensations, and these alone, patiently prospected, patiently exploited, came the inspirations and discoveries we should take care not to attribute to vague precedents of which he himself stood in complete ignorance.

CÉZANNE'S INFLUENCE

IN a letter to Leo Larguier, alluding to some of the younger painters, he wrote: "If they attempt to set up a school in my name, tell them they have never understood or cared for the things I have always worked towards."

Cézanne certainly had his reasons for issuing this warning. But there was no deflecting the course of events, and his impact on the art to come proved to be immense, indeed irreplaceable when we fully realize what the tenor of his message was. It took effect, unfortunately, along two quite different lines, readily distinguishable from each other but unequal in interest and scope. On the one hand we may trace the purely technical progeny his achievement fathered; on the other, much more far-reaching in its influence, is the aesthetic program behind it, which led to the epoch-making developments of modern art.

Cézanne's immediate influence was brought to bear on a number of younger men, all of whom may be summed up in the person of Gauguin. The latter, however, was far too strong a personality to follow meekly in anyone's tracks. Though his flair for decorative composition could hardly leave him indifferent to his elder's anti-impressionist discoveries, he took from these no more than their most superficial aspect, which was all that served his turn. This Cézanne resented and accused him, in quaint terms but with the utmost seriousness, of having "taken my sensations for a ride on all the ocean-going steamers." He could never stomach Gauguin's "ignorance of planes," his "neglect of modeling and shading." "He has never understood me," Cézanne complained, adding: "He's not a painter anyhow, but a maker of Chinese images."

The Nabis, for their part, loyal heirs of Impressionism that they were, entirely mistook the architectural function of Cézanne's color and merely appropriated his "modulations."

This is Cézanne's last picture, on which he was working when he died, and for him there remained much work to be done on it yet. His painting of the cottage proves that his obsession with geometry was never quite extinct, even in the final phase of his career when he seemed to have risen above every constraint imposed by technical considerations. These trees, on the other hand, the very stuff of poetry, show him rapturously sparing no element of form as he recasts them in accordance with his sense of color. What this picture proves, on the whole, is that up to the very end he was torn between the tyranny of the mind and that of the senses.

LE CABANON DE JOURDAN, 1906. (25 ½ × 31 ¾″)
KUNSTMUSEUM, BASEL.

last works, which are the summing-up of Cézanne's methods and conceptions; in them, forgetting the old obsession with architecture, he let his innate sense of color have its way, and it built the picture in terms of color harmonies with no need now of an initial geometric framework.

Only too often those who followed his lead missed the point and earnestly spent their energies in grafting geometry on forms willy-nilly in their zeal to wrench them from the context of traditional ways of seeing. Then, Cubism being in the air, they wantonly cleaved and sundered natural forms, reducing them to cubes without rhyme or reason, fancying this was enough to build a picture. As for those who saw in Cézanne the revolutionary he truly was, they were not blind to the fact that such building techniques as he had brought into prominence could also be detected in the work of Poussin, Corot and many others. What excited their enthusiasm were the genuinely original finds he had made and used in concert with his inspired continuation of time-honored techniques.

First of all came his fruitful practice of taking nature as the foodstuff of his inspiration, as it were, the rich and varied earth in which the flowers of his mind and senses—i.e. his pictures—might sink their roots and flourish. The great painters of our time have regarded Cézanne as above all a master-inventor, the creator of new forms who fired the best of the Cubists, together with those who profited from their experiments, with an epoch-making ambition: to create, on the basis of well-known natural elements, a new world of forms. For those who chose to follow him all the way, Cézanne was the inventor of a new perspective that left the old entirely where it seemed to him to belong: in the hands of sculptors, whose natural field of action is a three-dimensional one. He launched a notion of flat painting that Seurat described as "the art of hollowing out a surface." Thanks to Cézanne a new way of seeing was born, together with an aesthetic that at last delivered painting from the concept of nature-imitation laid down by Aristotle—an aesthetic, moreover, that added the correctives of the mind to the inadequate data of visual perspective, thereby lifting the mere tinglings of the senses to a sphere of pure thought. His achievement, in addition to this, was that of a master of color of such warmth, glow and seductive appeal as had rarely been seen in painting before.

In the legendary figure of Cézanne the younger men saw the stoic habitué of obscurity and solitude, and in his eyes the hunted look. They remembered the famous refrain of his conversation: "*Je ne veux pas qu'on me mette le grappin dessus.*" But he need never have feared; no one ever succeeded in "getting their hooks into him," and he takes his place in noble company, beside those other stormy-tempered, independent spirits of Capricorn, who, astrologically speaking, are his brothers: Dante, Michelangelo, El Greco, Dostoievsky, Edgar Allan Poe, Berlioz, Tolstoy. At any rate, if the certainties he brought to light amid so much uncertainty have met with such favor from later painters, the reason is that, in their eyes, Cézanne dared everything, like a hero of fable who sets out to steal the thunder of the gods and by some miracle, succeeds in his perilous venture.

SELECTED BIBLIOGRAPHY

EXHIBITIONS

INDEX OF PICTURES AND NAMES

CONTENTS

SELECTED BIBLIOGRAPHY

Writings by the Artist

Correspondance, over 200 letters, edited by J. REWALD, Paris 1937. English edition: *Letters*, London 1941.

Catalogue

L. VENTURI, *Cézanne, son art, son œuvre*, 2 vols., Paris 1936. Standard work. Catalogue listing 1634 items (805 paintings) with 1619 illustrations, a critical study and a complete bibliography (561 publications). A new, revised and enlarged edition is in active preparation.

Reminiscences

E. ZOLA, *Correspondance*, Paris 1907. — E. BERNARD, *Souvenirs sur Paul Cézanne et lettres inédites*, in *Mercure de France*, October 1 and 15, 1907. — A. VOLLARD, *Paul Cézanne*, Paris 1914; new edition, Paris 1919. In German, Munich 1921. In English: *Paul Cézanne, his Life and Art*, New York 1926. — K. OSTHAUS, article in *Das Feuer*, 1920; French translation in *Marianne*, February 22, 1939. — E. JALOUX, *Souvenirs sur Paul Cézanne*, in *L'Amour de l'Art*, 1920. — M. LAFARGUE, *Souvenirs sur Cézanne*, in *L'Amour de de l'Art*, January 1921. — C. CAMOIN, *Souvenirs sur Paul Cézanne* in *L'Amour de l'Art*, January 1921. — J. GASQUET, *Cézanne*, Paris 1921. — E. BERNARD, *Souvenirs sur Paul Cézanne*, Paris, 1921, 1925, 1926. — L. LARGUIER, *Le dimanche avec Paul Cézanne*, Paris 1925. — C. PISSARRO, *Lettres à son fils Lucien*, Paris 1950.

Monographs and Appraisals

E. BERNARD, *Paul Cézanne*, Les Hommes d'aujourd'hui, Paris 1892. — J. MEIER-GRAEFE, *Cézanne und seine Ahnen*, Munich 1910. — J. RIVIÈRE, *Cézanne*, 1910. — E. FAURE, *Paul Cézanne*, Paris 1910. — O. MIRBEAU, T. DURET, L. WERTH, F. JOURDAIN, *Cézanne*, Paris 1914. — M. DENIS, *Théories*, Paris 1912. — G. COQUIOT, *Paul Cézanne*, Paris 1919. — J. MEIER-GRAEFE, *Cézanne und sein Kreis*, Munich 1922. — G. RIVIÈRE, *Le maître Paul Cézanne*, Paris 1923. — T. KLINGSOR, *Cézanne*, Paris 1923. —

A. SALMON, *Cézanne*, Paris 1923. — J. MEIER-GRAEFE, *Cézanne*, London-New York 1927. — R. FRY, *Cézanne, a Study of his Development*, London 1927. — K. PFISTER. *Cézanne: Gestalt, Werk, Mythos*, Potsdam 1927. — E. D'ORS, *Cézanne*, Paris 1930; in English, London 1936. — G. MACK, *Paul Cézanne*, New York 1935. — M. RAYNAL, *Cézanne*, Paris 1936. — R. HUYGHE, *Cézanne*, Paris 1936. — J. REWALD, *Cézanne et Zola*, Paris 1936. — F. NOVOTNY, *Cézanne*, New York and Vienna 1937. — A. CHAPPUIS, *Dessins de Paul Cézanne*, Paris 1938. — F. NOVOTNY, *Cézanne und das Ende der wissenschaftlichen Perspektive*, Vienna 1938. — A. C. BARNES and V. DE MAZIA, *The Art of Cézanne*, New York 1939. — G. JEDLICKA, *Cézanne*, Zurich and Leipzig 1939. — M. RAYNAL, *Cézanne*, Paris and Geneva 1939; in English, Geneva and New York 1947, 1950. — J. REWALD, *Paul Cézanne, sa vie, son œuvre, son amitié pour Zola*, Paris 1939. — L. VENTURI, *Paul Cézanne, Water Colours*, London 1943. — E. LORAN, *Cézanne's Composition*, Berkeley and Los Angeles 1943. — R. M. RILKE, *Lettres sur Cézanne*, Paris 1944. — E. A. JEWELL, *Cézanne*, New York 1944. — P. M. AUZAS, *Peintures de P. Cézanne*, Paris 1945. — G. SCHILDT, *Le comportement psychologique de Cézanne, interprétation de son art et de sa personnalité*, Stockholm 1946. — B. DORIVAL, *Cézanne*, Paris 1948. — A. LHOTE, *Cézanne*, Lausanne 1949. — L. GUERRY, *Cézanne et l'expression de l'espace*, Paris 1950. — F. JOURDAIN, *Cézanne*, Paris 1950. — J. REWALD, *Paul Cézanne, Carnets de Dessins*, Paris 1951. — G. SCHMIDT, *Aquarelles de Paul Cézanne*, Basel 1952. — H. L. SCHERMAN, *Cézanne and Visual Form*, Ohio State University, Columbus 1952. — B. DORIVAL, *Cézanne*, Paris 1952. — M. SCHAPIRO, *Cézanne*, New York 1952. — T. ROUSSEAU, *Cézanne*, Paris 1954.

Chief Magazine Articles

L. LEROY, *L'exposition des impressionnistes*, in *Charivari*, April 25, 1874. — G. RIVIÈRE, *L'exposition des impressionnistes*, in *L'impressionniste, Journal d'Art*, April 14, 1877. — J. K. HUYSMANS, *Trois peintres, Cézanne, Tisson, Wagner*, in *La Cravache*, August 4, 1888: reprinted in *Certains*, 1889. — G. GEFFROY, *Paul Cézanne*, in *Le Journal*, March 25, 1894. — T. NATANSON, *Paul Cézanne*, in *Revue Blanche*, December 1, 1895. — A. FONTAINAS, *Exposition Cézanne*, in *Mercure de France*, June 1898. — F. FAGUS, *Quarante tableaux de Cézanne*, in *Revue Blanche*, December 15, 1899. — G. LECOMTE, *Paul Cézanne*, in *Revue d'Art*, December 9, 1899. — E. BERNARD, *Paul Cézanne*, in *L'Occident*, July 1904. — M. DENIS, *Cézanne*, in *L'Ermitage*, November 15, 1905. — J. ROYÈRE, *Sur Paul Cézanne*, in *La Phalange*, November 15, 1906. — M. DENIS, *Cézanne*, in *L'Occident*, September 1907. — C. MORICE, *Cézanne*, in *Mercure de France*, February 15, 1907. — R. RIVIÈRE and J. F. SCHNERB, *L'atelier de Cézanne*, in *La Grande Revue*, December 25, 1907. — A. ALEXANDRE, *L'œuvre de Paul Cézanne*, in

Comoedia, January 15, 1910. — M. DENIS, *Cézanne*, in *The Burlington Magazine*, January and February 1911. — E. FAURE, *Paul Cézanne*, in *L'Art Décoratif*, October 5, 1911. — A. GLEIZES, *La tradition et le cubisme*, in *Montjoie!*, February 1913. — E. BERNARD, *La méthode de Paul Cézanne*, in *Mercure de France*, March 1920. — A. LHOTE, *La méthode de Paul Cézanne*, in *Nouvelle Revue Française*, November 1920. — A. TABARANT, *Cézanne*, in *Bulletin de la Vie Artistique*, August 1921. — G. SEVERINI, *Cézanne et le cézannisme*, in *Esprit nouveau*, November and December 1921. — M. J. FRIEDLÄNDER, *Über Paul Cézanne*, in *Die Kunst*, February 1922. — E. BERNARD, *Les aquarelles de Cézanne*, in *L'Amour de l'Art*, February 1924. — M. DENIS, *Le dessin de Cézanne*, in *L'Amour de l'Art*, February 1924. — G. RIVIÈRE, *La formation de Paul Cézanne*, in *L'Amour de l'Art*, August 1, 1925. — J. G. GOULINAT, *L'évolution du métier de Cézanne*, in *L'Art Vivant*, March 1, 1925. — R. FRY, *Le développement de Cézanne*, in *L'Amour de l'Art*, December 1926. — F. NOVOTNY, *Paul Cézanne*, in *Belvedere*, 1929, No. 12. — J. REWALD and L. MARSCHUTZ, *Cézanne und der Jas de Bouffan*, in *Forum*, 1935, No. 9. — L. VENTURI, *Paul Cézanne*, in *L'Arte* 1935. — L. GILLET, *Le mystère Cézanne*, in *Revue des Deux Mondes*, 1936. — A. LHOTE, *Cézanne l'incompris*, in *Nouvelle Revue Française*, 1936. — L. DOUGLAS, *Paul Cézanne*, in *The Burlington Magazine*, 1936. — E. D'ORS, *Crise de Cézanne*, in *Gazette des Beaux-Arts*, 1936, I. — L. VENTURI, *Sur les dernières années de Cézanne*, in *Minotaure* 1936, No. 9. — L. VENTURI, *The Early Style of Cézanne*, in *Parnassus*, March 1937. — J. REWALD, *A propos du catalogue raisonné de l'œuvre de Cézanne et de la chronologie de cette œuvre*, in *La Renaissance*, March-April 1937. — A. BARR, *Cézanne d'après les lettres de Marion à Morstatt*, in *Gazette des Beaux-Arts*, 1937. — J. REWALD, *Achille Emperaire, ami de P. Cézanne*, in *L'Amour de l'Art*, May 1938. — G. BAZIN, *Cézanne et la Montagne Sainte-Victoire*, in *L'Amour de l'Art*, June 1938. — D. LEBLOND-ZOLA, *Paul Alexis, ami des peintres*, in *Mercure de France*, March 1939. — J. REWALD, *Paul Cézanne: New Documents on the Years 1870-1871*, in *Burlington Magazine*, April 1939. — F. B. DEKNATEL, *Manet and the Formation of Cézanne's Art*, in *College Art Journal* March 1942. — K. BADT, *Cézanne's Technique*, in *Burlington Magazine*, October 1943. — G. BAZIN, *Cézanne devant l'impressionnisme*, in *Labyrinthe*, February 15, 1945. — M. MERLEAU-PONTY, *Le doute de Cézanne*, in *Temps Modernes*, 1946. — J. BOUCHOT-SAUPIQUE, *Un carnet de croquis de Cézanne*, in *La Revue des Arts*, 1951.

Special Issues: *Mercure de France*, August 1, 1905. — *L'Amour de l'Art*, December 1920 (M. Denis, E. Faure, J. Gasquet, E. Jaloux, S. Lévy), January 1921 (C. Camoin, W. George, M. Lafargue), May 1936 (R. Huyghe and J. Rewald). — *La Renaissance*, May-June 1936 (P. Jamot, J. Combe, C. Sterling, J. Vergnet-Ruiz, C. Tolnay). — *L'Art Sacré*, May 1936 (M. Denis, J. Rewald, H. Héraut). — *Le Point*, August 1936, *Cézanne et la Provence* (J. Rewald, L. Marschutz).

EXHIBITIONS

Salon des Refusés, Paris, 1863. — First Group Exhibition of the Impressionists (3 canvases), Paris, April-May 1874. — Third Group Exhibition of the Impressionists (13 canvases, 3 watercolors), Paris, April 1877. — Salon (a portrait), Paris 1882. — Exhibition of "Les Vingt," Brussels 1887. — "Exposition Décennale" at the Paris World's Fair, 1889. — Gal. Vollard (over 150 canvases), Paris, November-December 1895; May-June 1898; December 1899. — Salon des Indépendants, Paris, 1899, 1901, 1902, 1905. — Centennial Exhibition of French Art (3 canvases), Paris 1900. — "La Libre Esthétique" Exhibition, Brussels 1901, 1904. — Salon d'Automne (Cézanne Room, 33 items), Paris 1904; 1905 (10 canvases); 1906 (10 canvases); 1907 (Retrospective, 57 items). — Gal. Bernheim-Jeune (79 watercolors), Paris, June 1907; January 1910 (68 canvases and watercolors); January 1914 (30 paintings); December 1920 (33 paintings, watercolors and drawings); December 1922; March 1924; June 1926 (Retrospective, 58 paintings and 99 watercolors); April 1935 (watercolors); May-June 1939 (Homage to Cézanne). — 12th International Art Exhibition (Cézanne Room), Venice 1920. — Kunsthalle, Basel, February 1921; August-October 1936 (173 items). — Cassirer Gallery, Berlin, November-December 1921. — Wildenstein Gallery, New York, January 1928. — Gal. Pigalle (43 canvases), Paris 1929. — Pennsylvania Museum of Art, Philadelphia, November-December 1934. — Gal. Renou et Colle (watercolors and bathing scenes), Paris, June 1935. — Reid and Lefebvre Gallery, London, July 1935; June 1937 (29 canvases and watercolors). — Musée de l'Orangerie (catalogue by C. Sterling, foreword by J. E. Blanche, preface by P. Jamot, 184 items), Paris 1936. — Bignou Gallery, New York, November-December 1936. — Museum of Art, San Francisco, September-October 1937. — Gal. Henriette (drawings), Paris, November-December 1938. — Gal. Paul Rosenberg (preface by A. Tabarant, 35 items), Paris, February-April 1939. — Rosenberg and Helft Gallery, London, April 1939. — Wildenstein Gallery (46 canvases, 70 watercolors, 20 drawings), London, June-July 1939. — Centenary of the Independent Painter Paul Cézanne, Société des Artistes Indépendants (preface by Maurice Denis, 24 canvases, 38 watercolors and drawings), Paris 1939. — Musée de Lyon (42 canvases, 17 watercolors, 19 drawings), 1939. — Mary Harriman Gallery, London, November-December 1939. — Bignou Gallery (watercolors), London, April 1940. — Galerie de France, Paris, January-February 1947. — Wildenstein Gallery, New York, April 1947. — Art Museum, Cincinnati, February-March 1947. — Art Institute, Chicago, February-March 1952; Metropolitan Museum of Art, New York, April-May 1952. — Monticelli and Provençal Baroque, Musée de l'Orangerie 23 Cézannes), June-September 1953. — Aix-en-Provence, Nice, Grenoble Catalogue by J. Leymarie, 50 items), July-September 1953. — Homage to Cézanne, Musée de l'Orangerie, (73 items), Paris 1954.

INDEX OF PICTURES REPRODUCED AND MENTIONED

At each stage of his development Cézanne worked and reworked at more or less the same set of themes. To bring this out, and to facilitate research-work and comparisons, we here append (1) a chronological list, by subject-headings, of pictures reproduced and (2) a second list, similarly arranged, of pictures mentioned in the text. In brackets after each picture-title appears the corresponding number assigned it by Lionello Venturi in his catalogue of Cézanne's works. Page-numbers in roman type refer to the colorplates.

PICTURES REPRODUCED

LANDSCAPES

STILL LIFES

PORTRAITS AND FIGURE-PAINTINGS

NUDES

LARGE FIGURE-SCENES

COPY

PICTURES MENTIONED

LANDSCAPES

PORTRAITS AND FIGURE-PAINTINGS

LARGE FIGURE-SCENES

COPIES, EARLY WORKS

INDEX

CONTENTS

ON THE TITLE PAGE:

Self-Portrait, 1883-1887. (17½×14″) Ny Carlsberg Glyptotek, Copenhagen.

THIS VOLUME, THE EIGHTH OF THE COLLECTION "THE TASTE
OF OUR TIME," WAS PRODUCED BY THE TECHNICAL STAFF OF
EDITIONS D'ART ALBERT SKIRA, FINISHED THE THIRTIETH DAY
OF   SEPTEMBER   NINETEEN   HUNDRED   AND   FIFTY-FOUR

TEXT AND ILLUSTRATIONS BY

COLOR STUDIO
AT IMPRIMERIES RÉUNIES S.A., LAUSANNE.

PLATES ENGRAVED BY
GUEZELLE ET RENOUARD, PARIS.

PHOTOGRAPHS

*The works reproduced in this volume were photographed by Louis Laniepce, Paris
(pages 18, 19, 20, 27, 29, 34, 35, 46, 51, 80, 82, 102, 106), Hans Hinz, Basel
(pages 21, 52, 53, 59, 103, 111, 121, back of jacket), Henry B. Beville, Washington
(pages 12, 23, 31, 33, 39, 42, 49, 55, 65, 66, 75, 77, 83, 85, 87, 89, 91, 98, 104),
Frank Lerner, New York (pages 68, 72, 107, 115), courtesy of the Ny Carlsberg
Glyptotek, Copenhagen (pages 3 and 57), courtesy of the National Gallery, Oslo
(page 84), courtesy of the magazine Du, Zurich (pages 40, 41, 109), courtesy of the
Istituto d'Arti grafiche, Bergamo (pages 44 and 69).*